접외풍경의 노래

세월 밖 이야기

겁외풍경의 노래
세월 밖 이야기

2024년 12월 20일 초판 인쇄
2024년 12월 25일 초판 발행

글·그림 허허당 | 펴낸이 이찬규
펴낸곳 북코리아 | 등록번호 제03-01240호
전화 02-704-7840 | 팩스 02-704-7848
이메일 ibookorea@naver.com | 홈페이지 www.북코리아.kr
주소 13209 경기도 성남시 중원구 사기막골로45번길 14 우림2차 A동 1007호
ISBN 979-11-94299-11-0 (03220)
값 29,800원

세월 밖 이야기

겹외풍경의 노래

허허당

북코리아

목차

깨달음의 춤(禪舞) 화선지에 먹, 727×119cm, 2022
Dances of enlightment (禪舞) Ink on rice paper, 727×119cm, 2022

새가 날개를 펴면 허공이 새의 놀이터이듯
사람은 마음을 펴면 천하가 놀이터이다.

Just as the open air is a playground for a bird which has spread its wings,
The vast world can be a playground for a man who has opened up his heart.

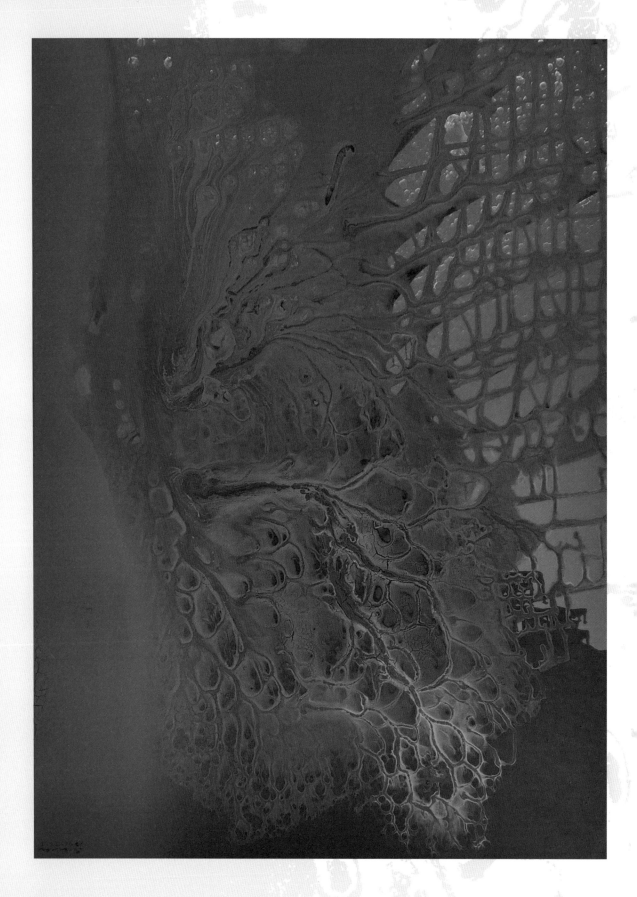

창조적인 사람은

창조적인 사람은 경쟁하지 않는다.
경쟁하는 삶은 주어진 삶을 쫓는 것일 뿐
진실로 자신의 삶을 사는 그것이 아니다.

창조적인 사람은
오직 스스로 닦아 세상을 비춰볼 뿐
아무하고도 경쟁하지 않는다.

Creative beings

Creativity does not originate from competition.
A life of competition is only about chasing a given life,
not living it to our fullest.

A creative man views the world only through his own glasses,
not by endless competition with others.

우주의 심장

살아 있다는 것은 세상을 아름답게 보라는 것.
죽는다는 것은 그 아름다움을 품으라는 것.
지금 내가 살아 있는 것은 우주의 심장이
뛰고 있는 것.

Heart of the Cosmos

To be alive means to see the world with beauty,
To die means to embrace that beauty.
The very fact that I am alive in this moment,
is to feel the heart of the universe,
pulsating through the cosmos.

겁외풍경 – 우주의 심장 캔버스에 혼합물감, 65.2×91cm, 2022
'Landscapes beyond time (겁외풍경)' – Heart of the Cosmos   Mixed media on canvas, 65.2×91cm, 2022

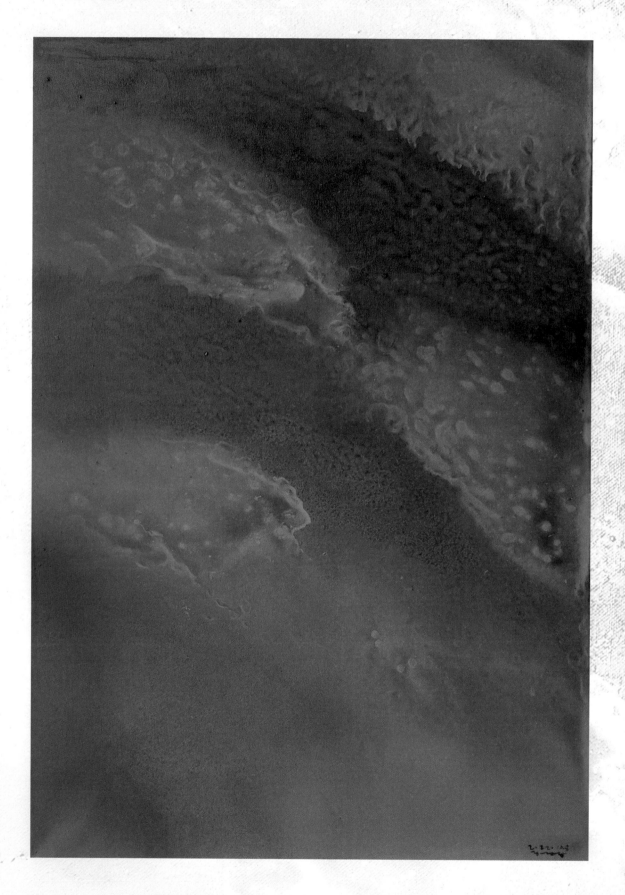

14

온전한 삶의 자유

인생은 머뭇거리는 것이 아니다. 인생은 곧 사는 것이다.
바로바로 살아야 사는 맛이 나지 두고두고 살면 사는 맛이 안 난다.
온전한 삶의 자유는 그것이 무엇이든 있는 그대로 살아버리는 것,
통쾌하게 탁탁- 뒷일 남기지 않고.

Freedom of life

Life is not about hesitation; life is to live fully, at its very moment.
One must seize the moment, for delaying dulls the taste of our existence.
True freedom in life lies in embracing everything as it is.
Living boldy and decisively - with no lingering shadows left behind.

겹외풍경 - 열정 캔버스에 혼합물감, 72.7×100cm, 2022
'Landscapes beyond time (겹외풍경)' - Passion Mixed media on canvas, 72.7×100cm, 2022

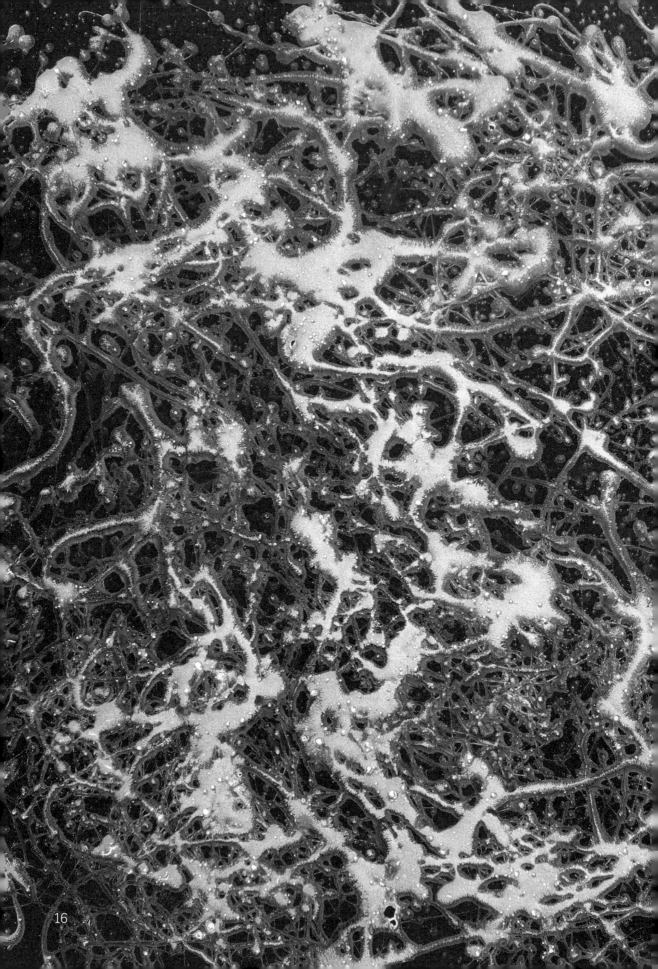

16

겁외풍경 – 베토벤의 영감   캔버스에 혼합물감, 80.3×100cm, 2022
'Landscapes beyond time (겁외풍경)' – Inspirations of Beethoven   Mixed media on canvas,
80.3×100cm, 2022

소리와 악기

좋은 악기는 좋은 소리를 내지만
절대 소리를 붙잡지 않는다.
그대가 만약 좋은 악기처럼 산다면
세상 그 무엇에도 걸림 없을 것이다.

소리는 악기에 머물지 않고
악기는 소리를 붙잡지 않는다.

Sounds and instruments

Fine instruments produce beautiful sounds,
yet never holds them in it's place.
Shall we live like a noble instrument,
nothing in the world will hold us back.

Sound flows freely, never lingering in the instrument,
The instrument, in turn, does not grasp the sound.

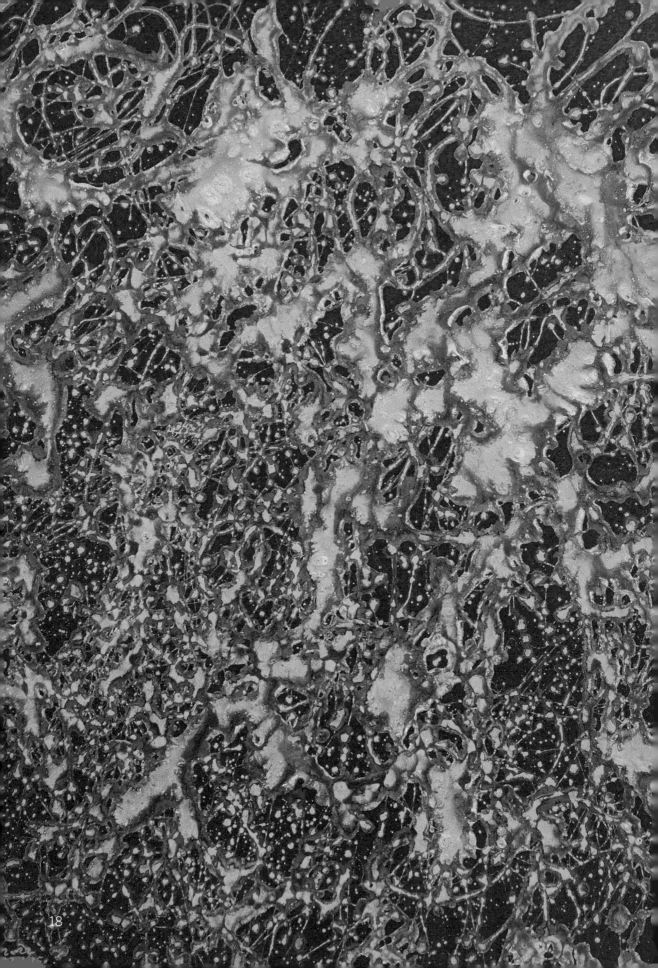

18

울림

우리네 삶은
매 순간 울림의 연속이다.
태어남도 울림이요 죽음 또한 울림이다.
우리네 인생은 매 순간 울림을 통해
성장하고 깨닫고 본래 자리로 돌아간다.
울림!
오늘 하루 그대는 어떤 울림을 가졌는가?

Echos

Our lives are,
a continuous echo in every moment.
Birth is an echo, and so is death.
Through each resonance, we grow, awaken, and eventually,
return to our true place.
Echo!
Today, what resonance have we embraced?

겹외풍경 – 모차르트의 영감   캔버스에 혼합물감, 80.3×100cm, 2022
'Landscapes beyond time (겹외풍경)' – Inspirations of Mozart   Mixed media on canvas,
80.3×100cm, 2022

생명의 축제 – Chuck Mangione, 산체스의 아이들 80×119.2cm, 2001
Festival of life – Chuck Mangione, Children of Sanchez 80×119.2cm, 2001

세상이 내 눈앞에 있는 것은

인생은 노는 것이다,
하고 싶은 일을 하며 가슴 뛰게.
이 세상이 내 눈앞에 펼쳐진 것은
하고 싶은 일을 하며 가슴 뛰게 놀라는 것.
다른 의미가 아니다.

The world unfolds before my eyes

Life is all about frolics;
choosing to do what sets our heart racing.
The world unfolds before my eyes,
a wonder sparked by the joy of pursuing my desires,
no deeper meaning shall lie beyond this delight.

기적

기적은 반드시 그대가 모르는 곳에서 일어나며
그대가 아는 것은 이미 기적이 아니다.
만약 그대가 기적을 원한다면 그냥 아무것도 모르는 채 살아라.
그리하면 기적이 자주 일어날 것이다.

Miracles

Miracles arise from palces we do not know of;
what we know are no longer miracles.
Shall we seek the miraculous, we must live in a state of delightful ignorance.
Then, we shall witness those miracles unfold.

겹외풍경 – 줄탁동시(존재의 기쁨) 캔버스에 혼합물감, 80.3×100cm, 2023
'Landscapes beyond time (겹외풍경)' – 'Jultak-Dongsi' (Joy of existence) Mixed media on canvas, 80.3×100cm, 2023

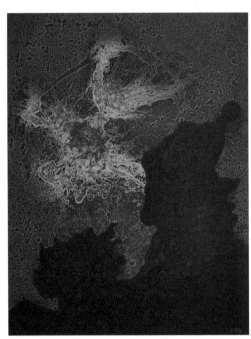

겹외풍경 – 가릉빈가의 노래
캔버스에 혼합물감, 91×116.8cm, 2023
'Landscapes beyond time (겹외풍경)' – Hymns of Kalavinka
Mixed media on canvas, 91×116.8cm, 2023

내 안에 없는 것은

지금 그대가 찾는 것은 이미 그대 안에 있다.
두드리면 열리는 것이 아니라 이미 열려 있다.
가라, 아무런 두려움 없이.
내 안에 없는 것은 죽어도 없다.
모든 것은 이미 내 안에 있다.

What lies beyond within me

What we seek for is already within ourselves.
It does not open with a knock; for it is already ajar.
Go forth, fearlessly; for nothing exists outside of myself.
All is already within.

겁외풍경 – 불새   캔버스에 혼합물감, 80.3×116.8cm, 2023
'Landscapes beyond time (겁외풍경)' – Firebird   Mixed media on canvas, 80.3×116.8cm, 2023

절대 자유의 삶

절대 자유의 삶 속에는 절대 변명의 여지가 없다.
지금 그대가 삶의 어떤 순간에도
아무런 변명 없이 나아갈 수 있다면
그대는 이미 자유인이다.

Absolute freedom of life

In a life of absolute freedom, lies no room for excuses.
If in the state of our current lives,
we are to go on without justification,
our souls have already been freed.

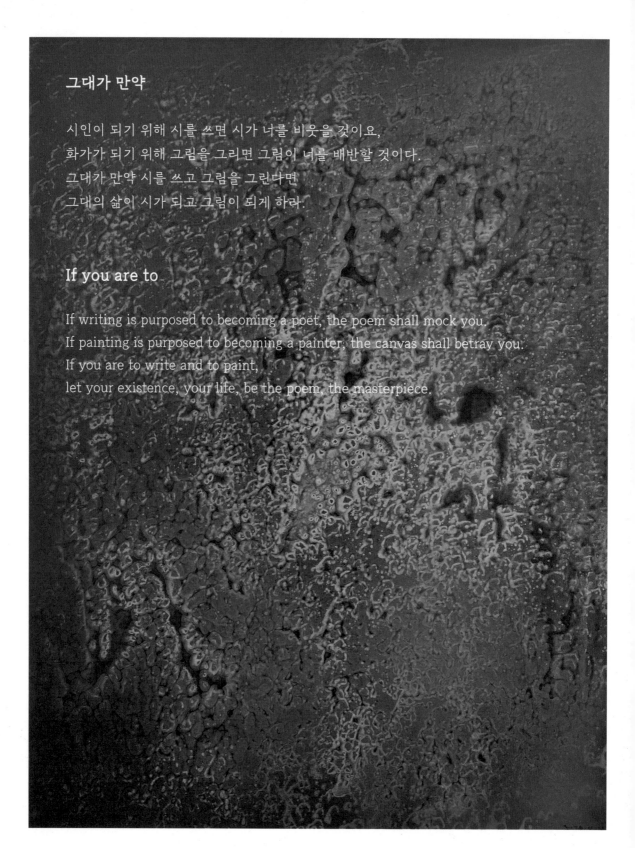

그대가 만약

시인이 되기 위해 시를 쓰면 시가 너를 비웃을 것이요,
화가가 되기 위해 그림을 그리면 그림이 너를 배반할 것이다.
그대가 만약 시를 쓰고 그림을 그린다면
그대의 삶이 시가 되고 그림이 되게 하라.

If you are to

If writing is purposed to becoming a poet, the poem shall mock you.
If painting is purposed to becoming a painter, the canvas shall betray you.
If you are to write and to paint,
let your existence, your life, be the poem, the masterpiece.

겁외풍경 – 피카소의 꿈 캔버스에 혼합물감, 91×116.8cm, 2023
'Landscapes beyond time (겁외풍경)' – Dreams of Picasso   Mixed media on canvas, 91×116.8cm, 2023

오직 인간만이

인간사 이외 모든 것은
시간도 없고 세월도 없다. 천당도 없고 지옥도 없다.
오직 인간만이 시간과 세월, 천당과 지옥을 두고
오직 인간만이 그것으로부터 자유롭지 못하다.

Only mankind

Beyond the realm of humanity,
there is neither time nor age, no heaven nor hell.
Only mankind grapple with time and seasons,
only they remain bound, unable to break free.

초조해하지 마라

오늘 하루 아무런 의미 없이 간다 해도
너무 초조해하지 마라.
아무런 의미 없이 간 하루도
지금 그대를 있게 한 중요한 시간이다.

Do not be anxious

Anxiety is not needed just because
today has passed by without meaning.
Meaningless days that have passed
are what makes us who we are today; for they are meaningful.

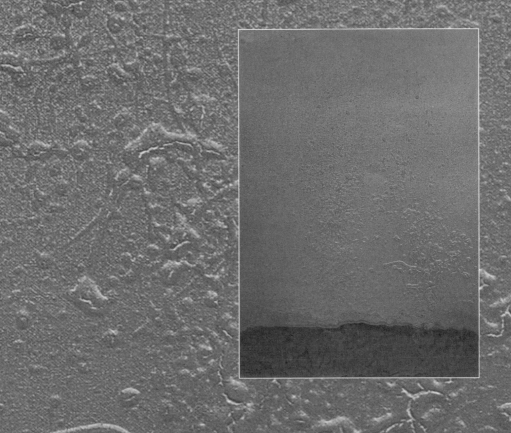

겁외풍경 – 저물녘 캔버스에 혼합물감, 80×100cm, 2023
'Landscapes beyond time〈겁외풍경〉' – Twilight   Mixed media on canvas, 80×100cm, 2023

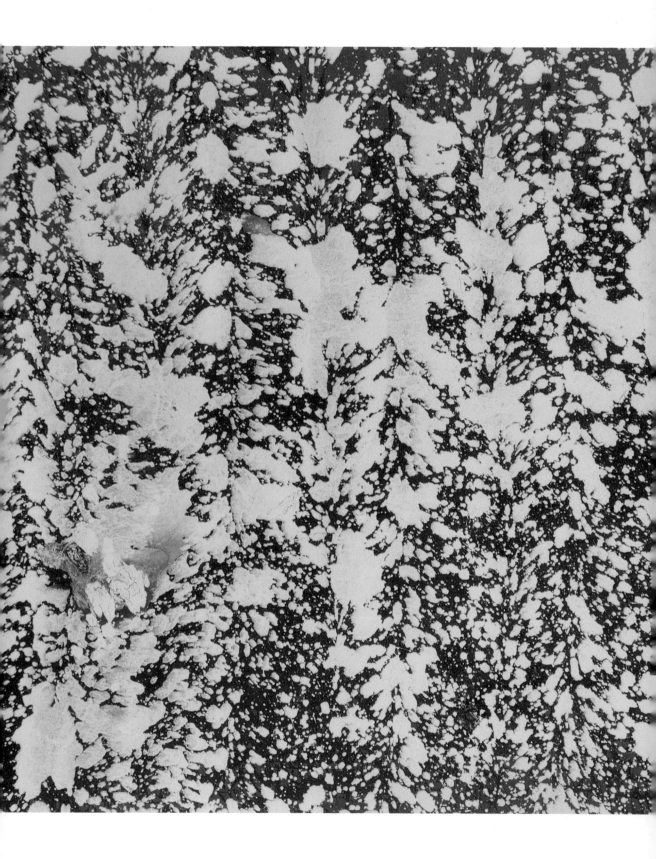

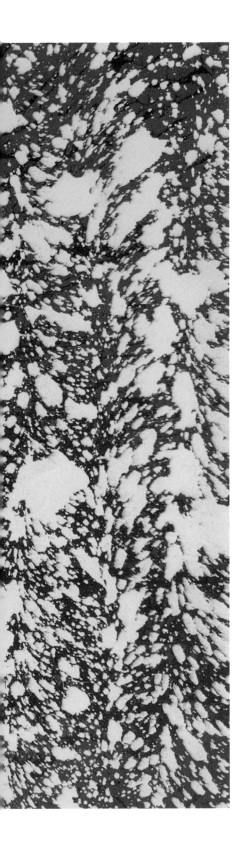

큰마음을 가진 자

자신의 존재를 잘 가지고 노는 사람은
세상 어디를 가도 자유롭다.
참으로 잘 사는 사람은 내 것 없이도 잘 사는 사람이다.
큰마음을 가진 자는 우주를 통째로 굴리기에
별도의 내 것을 만들지 않는다.

The one with a generous heart

Those who can be playful with their own existence
find freedom wherever they go.
The truly rich live well without possessions,
for the one with a generous heart
can embrace the cosmos whole,
creating nothing separate for themselves.

겁외풍경 – 생명의 꽃(화엄장) 캔버스에 혼합물감, 91×116.8cm, 2022
'Landscapes beyond time (겁외풍경)' – Flowers of life (Avatamsaka Sutra)
Mixed media on canvas, 91×116.8cm, 2022

여행의 끝은 없다, 삶이 곧 여행이기에.
죽어도 끝이 없다, 또 다른 여행이기에.

There is no end to travelling, for we journey through life.
Death is not an end, for it is a beginning of another long journey.

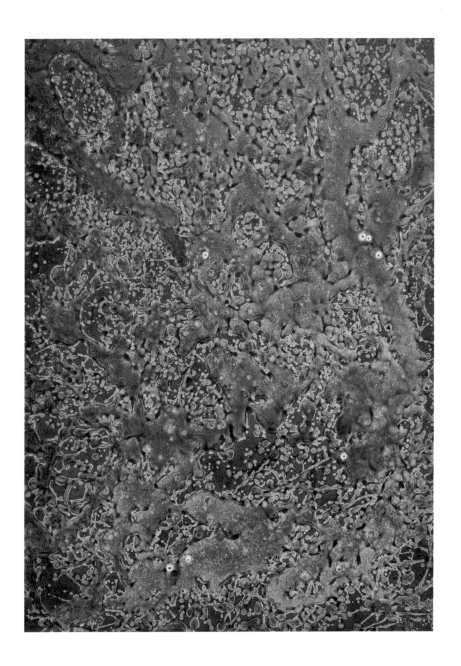

견외풍경의 북두칠성 캔버스에 혼합물감, 65.2×91cm, 2023
The Big Dipper of 'Landscapes beyond time (견외풍경)' Mixed media on canvas, 65.2×91cm, 2023

떠나 있어라.
떠나 있는 자에겐 삶이 곧 여행이다.
찾지 마라, 잃기 쉽다.

Embark.
Life is a journey for those who have set afar.
Do not go searching, it will be easy to get lost.

경외풍경 - 줄탁동시(존재의 슬픔) 캔버스에 혼합문감, 80.3×100cm, 2023
'Landscapes beyond time (경외풍경)' – 'Jultak-Dongsi' (Grief of existence) Mixed media on canvas, 80.3×100cm, 2023

머물지 마라 그 아픈 상처에

불이 나면 꺼질 일만 남고
상처가 나면 아물 일만 남는다.
머물지 마라, 그 아픈 상처에.

Do not stay at those painful wounds

A spark waits to be blown away,
A wound waits to be healed.
Do not stay at those painful wounds.

사막은 사람을 푸르게 한다

사막은 사람을 푸르게 한다.
풀 한 포기 없는 사막에선 사람 스스로 푸르더라.
두려워 마라, 그대가 지금 황량한 사막에 홀로 있어도
온 세상을 푸르게 할 수 있는 주인공이다.

The desert brings forth a verdant spirit

The desert brings forth a verdant spirit.
In a barren land, one can cultivate their own greenery.
Do not fear, for even in this desolate expanse,
you are the hero who can make the whole world bloom.

겁외풍경 – 지구의 탯줄 캔버스에 혼합물감, 65.2×91cm, 2022
'Landscapes beyond time (겁외풍경)' – Earth's umbilical cord   Mixed media on canvas, 65.2×91cm, 2022

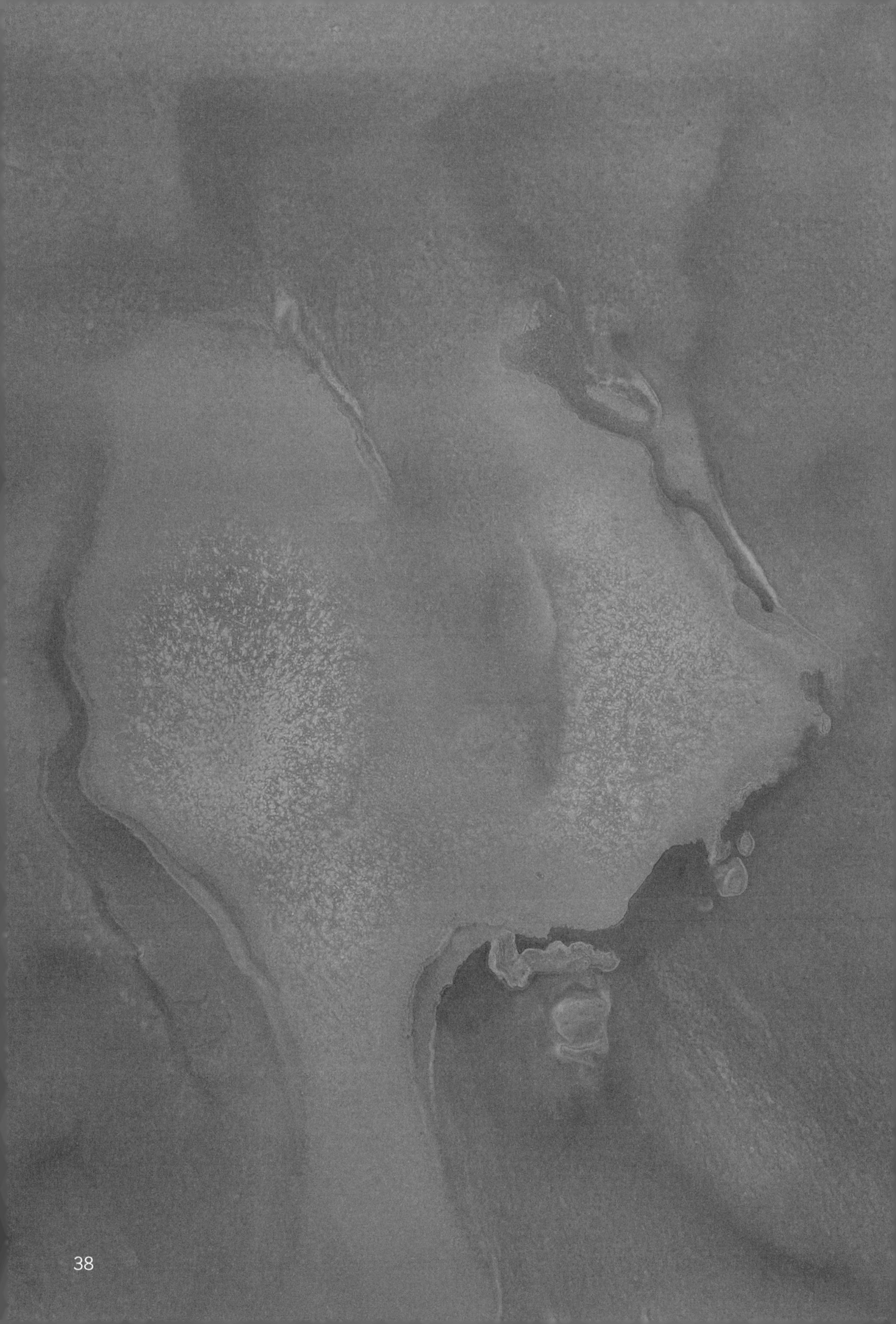

나의 그림은

살아 있는 모든 것은 존재 그 자체로,
이미 충분히 아름답고 놀랍고도 신비로운 예술임이 틀림없다.
나의 그림은 이 신비로운 생명 예술에 반응하며 춤추고 노래한다.
일체 생명의 자유와 아름다움 속에서.

My artworks

Everything of life is, without doubt,
already a beautiful and surprising, yet mysterious piece of art.
My artworks dance and sing in reactions to this art of life,
in the midst of the freedom and beauty of it.

겹외풍경 – 놀라움 설레임   캔버스에 혼합물감, 116.8×91cm, 2022
'Landscapes beyond time (겹외풍경)' – Amazement, Excitement   Mixed media on canvas, 116.8×91cm, 2022

허허당 초실존화 '겁외풍경'

허허당 초실존화는 우리 인간 인식의 한계를 넘어선 세계, 인간의 삶의 양식을 벗어난 일체 만물의 순수 생명활동, 생명의 근원에서 일어나는 온갖 소리와 빛 파장 등의 에너지를 캔버스에 담으며 참생명의 자유와 아름다움을 노래한다. 우주는 하나의 큰 생명 덩어리요, 세계는 하나의 큰 생명의 꽃이다. 초실존화는 모든 생명의 근원에 역점을 두면서 동시에 우주의 본질을 관(觀)하여 일체 생명을 품는다.

"겁외풍경(劫外風景)은 세월 밖의 세계"
세월은 안도 밖도 없지만 굳이 '겁외풍경', 즉 '세월 밖의 풍경'이라 이름한 것은 우리 인간의 지적 한계, 인식의 한계를 벗어난 광대무변한 우주법계의 생명활동을 표현하기 위해서다. 허허당 초실존화 겁외풍경은 지구가 탄생하기 이전의 세계, 인류가 존재하기 이전의 세계, 탄생의 순간, 혹은 갑자기 지구가 사라져버린 이후의 세계 등 끝없는 우주법계의 근원적 생명활동을 조명하는 것이다.

Huhhuhdang's 'Landscapes beyond time (겁외풍경),' a work of 'Super-existentialism.'

Huhhuhdang's 'Super-existentialism' transcends the limits of human perception, capturing the pure life activities of all beings that go beyond human ways of living. It embodies the energies of sounds and light waves originating from the source of life on the canvas, singing of the freedom and beauty of true life. The universe is a large mass of life, and the world is a grand flower of existence. Transcendental abstraction emphasizes the origin of all life while simultaneously observing the essence of the universe, embracing all forms of life.

"'Landscapes beyond time (겁외풍경)' depicts a world outside of time"
There is no inside or outside to time, but the name 'Landscapes beyond time (Guob-Oe)' was chosen in intention to express the vast and infinite activities of life in the cosmological world, outside of our intellectual capacity, and consciousness. Huhudang's 'Landscapes beyond time (Guob-Oe),' a work of 'super-exisentialism,' depicts a world before humanity existed, and the moment of birth, as well as an apocalytic world following the disappearance of the Earth.

겁외풍경 – 지구의 탄생 캔버스에 혼합물감, 72.7×100cm, 2022
'Landscapes beyond time (겁외풍경)' – The birth of Earth   Mixed media on canvas, 72.7×100cm, 2022

우주를 품은 아이 화선지에 수채화물감, 31×35cm, 2011
A child who embraces the universe Watercolor on rice paper, 31×35cm, 2011

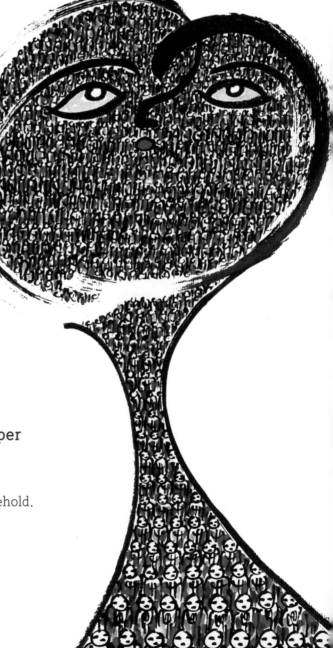

잠시 스쳐 지나갈 세상

너는 태어났다, 아무런 부족함 없이.
너는 온전했다, 무엇과도 비교할 수 없이.
어떠랴! 한 점 바람이면
잠시 스쳐 지나갈 세상.

The world will pass on by in a whisper

You were born, untouched and whole.
Unmatched in your perfection, a rarity to behold.
Oh, how fleeting! Like a whisper of wind,
A momentary brush with this world.

영혼의 텃밭

사막과 벌판, 황무지는 내 영혼의 텃밭이다.
사막에 서면 온 세상을 껴안을 힘이 생기고
벌판에 서면 온갖 생명을 사랑할 힘이 생긴다.
그리고 황무지에 서면 무한한 자비심이 샘솟는다.
겨울 산 겨울나무는 슬프게도 아름답다.
빈 나뭇가지가 바람에 흔들리면
내 안의 모든 것이 눈물이 된다.

The garden of my soul

The desert and the plains, the wastelands are the garden of my soul.
In the desert, I find the strength to embrace the world,
On the plains, the power to love all living things.
And in the wasteland, boundless compassion wells up.
The winter mountain, its trees adorned in sorrow,
When empty branches sway in the wind,
everything within me becomes a river of tears.

겁외풍경 – 오렌지 눈물 캔버스에 혼합물감, 91×116.8cm, 2022
'Landscapes beyond time (겁외풍경)' – Orange tears Mixed media on canvas, 91×116.8cm, 2022

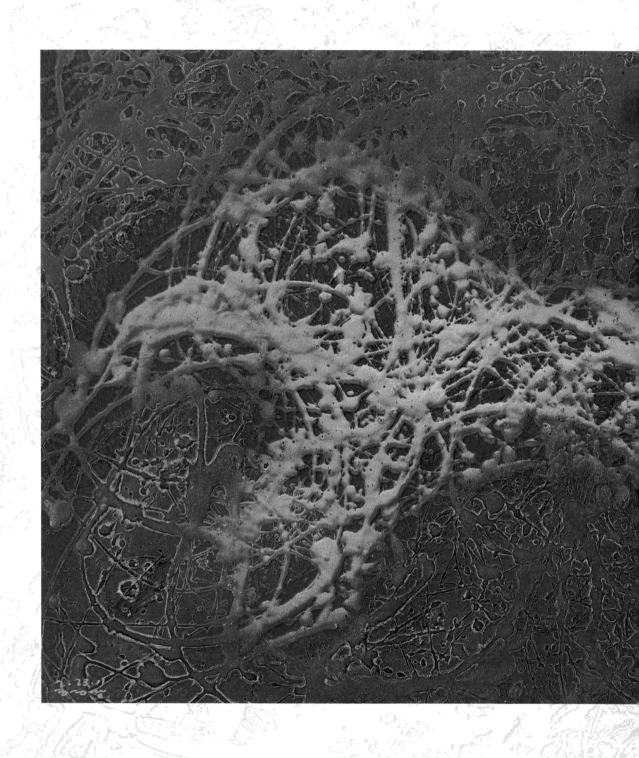

겁외풍경 – 자유 평화 사랑 캔버스에 혼합물감, 65×191cm, 2023
'Landscapes beyond time (겁외풍경)' – Freedom, Peace, Love   Mixed media on canvas, 65×191cm, 2023

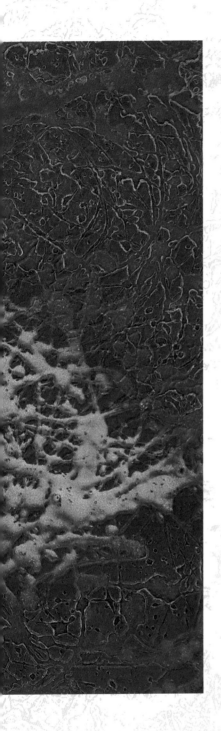

산중의 아침

산속의 아침은 푸른 나뭇잎에서 돋아나
새들의 입으로 사방으로 옮겨 가고
흰나비가 팔랑대며 고루고루 퍼터린다.
산중의 아침은 새소리가 밥이라
고요히 앉아 명상에 들면 배 절로 부르다.
솔밭에서 부는 바람 새소리에 치여 몸살을 한다.
가지에 숨은 빛들도 아무도 겁먹지 않고
잘난 체 않고 이기려 들지 않는다.
사람이 없는 숲은 모든 것이 평온하다.

Mornings in the mountains

Mornings in the mountains spring from green leaves,
carried by hymns of the birds to every corner.
as white butterflies fluttser, spreading joy all around.
In the mountain's dawn, the birdcalls are sustenance,
and as I sit in stillness, my heart fills with quiet hunger.
Winds blow through the pine forest,
stirred by melodies, bringing a gentle ache.
The lights hidden in the branches, undaunted,
neither boastful nor striving to conquer.
In the forest where no one treads, all is serene.

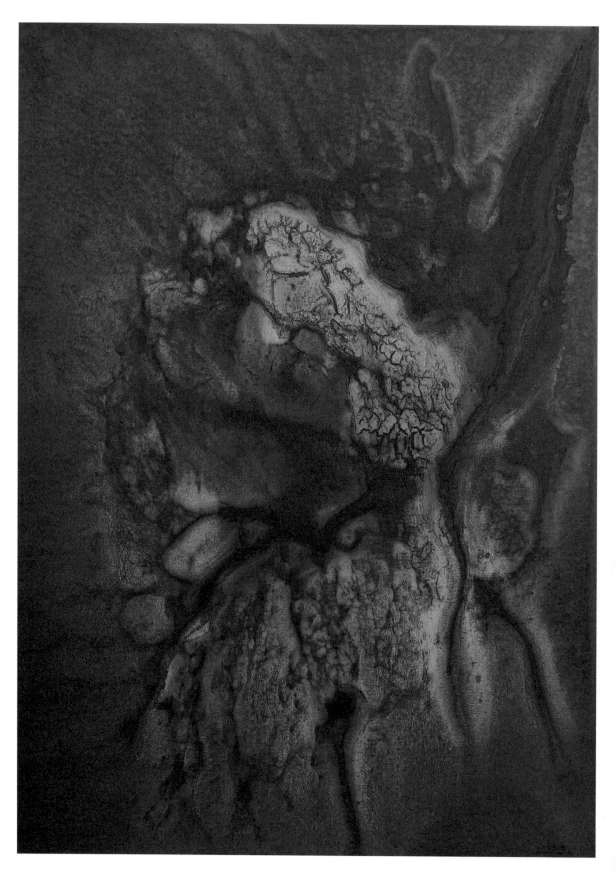

그런 사람

푸른빛이 감도는
윤기 나는 사고와 고독의 색이 독수리 눈 같은 사람,
쳐다만 봐도 가슴이 철렁 내려앉는 그런 사람이 그리운 날이다.
높은 하늘에 홀로 반짝이는 차가운 별빛 같은 사람.
가삿골 찬바람이 무릎을 차고
한 마리 산새가 알몸으로 난다.

Such a soul

On a day I long for someone,
A person with the hue of a blue light,
shining with the brilliance of thought and solitude,
whose gaze sends a tremor through my heart.
Like a cold star shimmering alone in the high sky,
a figure brushed by the sharp winds of winter,
while a mountain bird soars, naked and free.

겁외풍경 – 최초의 화석 인간   캔버스에 혼합물감, 65.2×91cm, 2022
'Landscapes beyond time (겁외풍경)' – The primordial fossil of humanity   Mixed media on canvas, 65.2×91cm, 2022

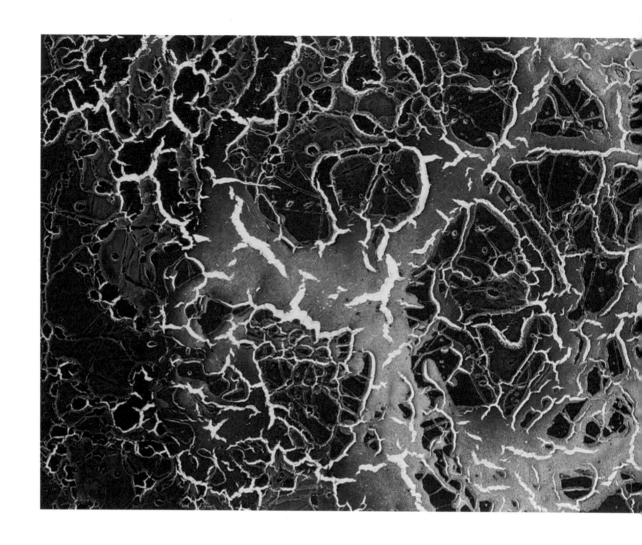

그대 겨울 밤에는

오직 한 가지 일에 몰입하는 사람,
그대 겨울밤에는 앙상한 뼈다귀로 서 있으라.
빈 나뭇가지가 우는 것처럼
그대 영혼을 울게 하라.

On a winter's night

To the one who dedicates fully to a single pursuit,
stand like a frail skeleton on a winter's night.
Let your soul weep,
like a barren branch lamenting in the cold.

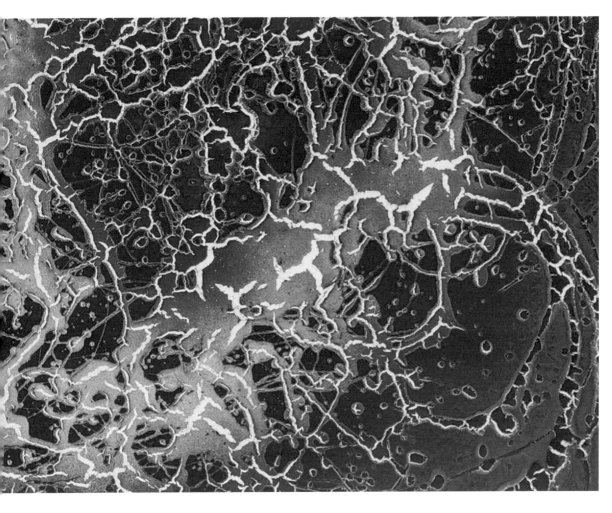

겁외풍경 – 깨어 있는 통증 캔버스에 혼합물감, 80.3×116.8cm, 2023
'Landscapes beyond time (겁외풍경)' – Awakened pain
Mixed media on canvas, 80.3×116.8cm, 2023

성공과 실패

인생을 성공과 실패로 가름한다면 태어남이 가장 큰 성공일 것이요,
동시에 죽음을 안고 나왔으니 이미 가장 큰 실패를 한 것이다.
이 도리를 아는 사람은 성공과 실패를 뛰어넘어 참나를 찾아간다.

Success and failure

If we were to measure the successes and failures of life,
birth would be our greatest triumph,
yet with death craded in our hands,
we have already faced the greatest defeat.
Those who grasp this truth
transcend success and failure,
seeking the true self beyond.

겁외풍경 – 빛의 노래 캔버스에 혼합물감, 91×116.8cm, 2022
'Landscapes beyond time (겁외풍경)' – Hymns of light Mixed media on canvas, 91×116.8cm, 2022

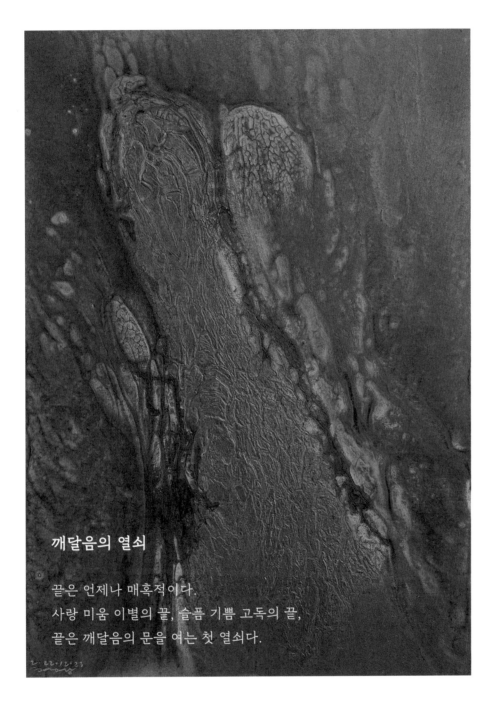

겁외풍경 - 화석 돌고래 캔버스에 혼합물감, 72.7×100cm, 2022
'Landscapes beyond time (겁외풍경)' - Fossilized dolphin Mixed media on canvas, 72.7×100cm, 2022

깨달음의 열쇠

끝은 언제나 매혹적이다.
사랑 미움 이별의 끝, 슬픔 기쁨 고독의 끝,
끝은 깨달음의 문을 여는 첫 열쇠다.

Keys to enlightenment

Ends are always enchanting.
The conclusion of love, hate, and parting.
The end of grief, joy and solitude.
Ends are the first steps toward doors to enlightenment.

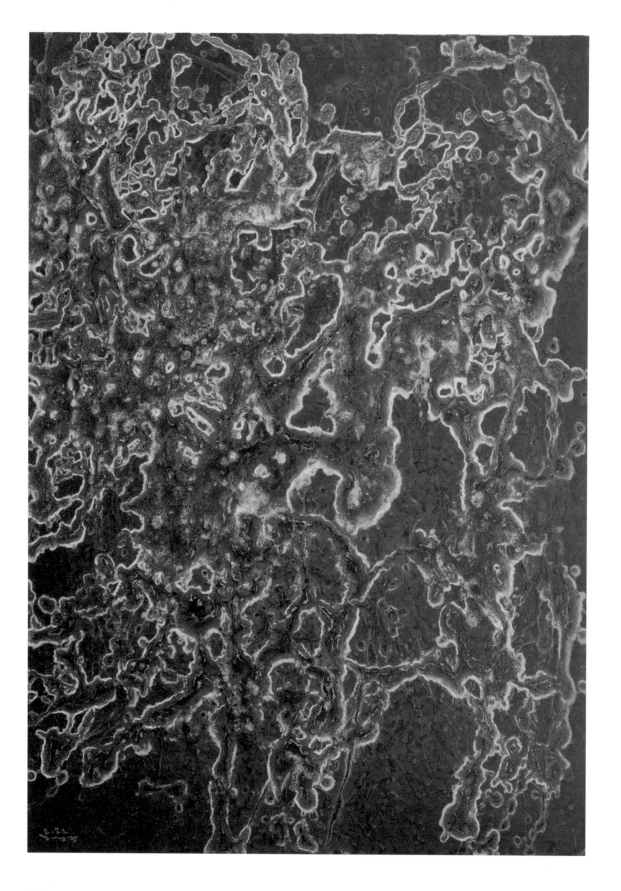

안심입명(安心立命)

지독하게 외롭고 고독한 삶 속에
얼척없이 아름다운 행복이 있다.

끝에서 끝을 보라.
고독의 끝, 외로움의 끝, 슬픔의 끝에서.
끝에서 끝을 봐야 안심입명이다.

A calm and clear mind (安心立命)

Inside a deeply lonesome life lies
happiness so bewildering and beautiful.

Look to the ends,
where solitude meets its edge,
where loneliness wanes, and sorrow fades;
only at the end can true peace be discerned.

겁외풍경 – Buddy Guy   캔버스에 혼합물감, 65.1×91cm, 2023
'Landscapes beyond time (겁외풍경)' – Buddy Guy   Mixed media on canvas, 65.1×91cm, 2023

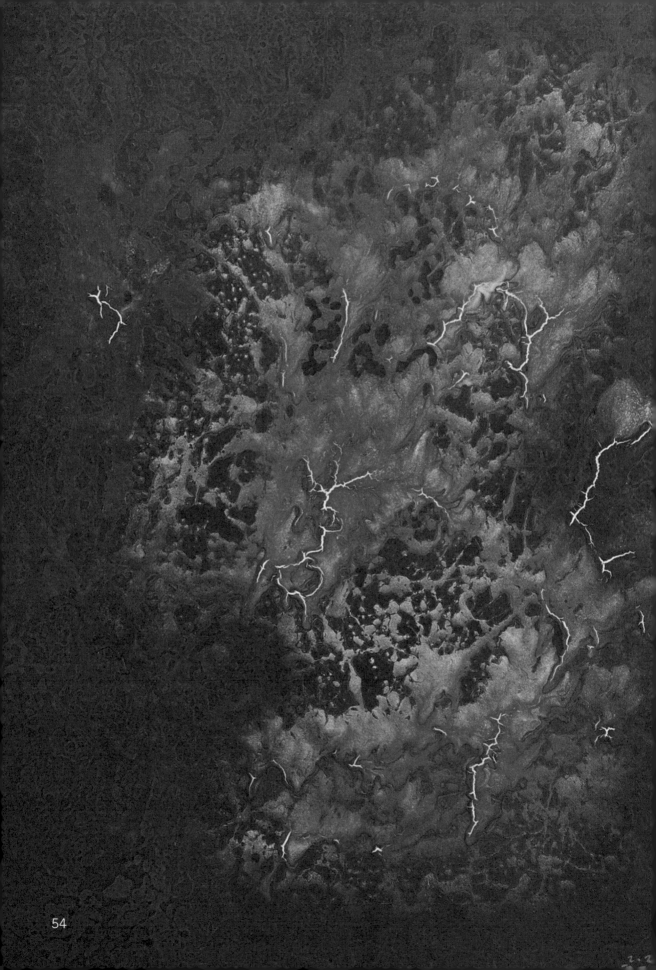

구제의 길

누가 나를 구제해 주길 바라지 마라.
그대는 이미 스스로를 구제할 능력이 충분하다.
자신을 구제할 사람은 오직 자신뿐이란 것을 알면
그대는 이미 깨달음의 길에 들어선 것이다.
스스로 구제받지 못한 이는 다른 어떤 누구도 구제할 수 없다.
부처도 예수도 오직 스스로 구제받은 사람이다.

Salvation

We must not wait for salvation,
for we possess within ourselves the strength to redeem ourself.
When you realize that only you can be your savior,
you have already stepped onto the path of enlightenment.
Those who cannot save themselves
cannot be saved by anyone else.
Even Buddha and Christ were solely those
who found redemption within.

겁외풍경 – HUHSPIRIT 1 캔버스에 혼합물감, 80.3×100cm, 2024
'Landscapes beyond time (겁외풍경)' – HUHSPIRIT 1   Mixed media on canvas, 80.3×100cm, 2024

무위자연

모였다 흩어졌다 다시 모인다.
산바람, 들바람, 강바람,
산기슭에 피어 있는 개나리꽃
노란 속삭임이 눈물겹다.
아무도 오지 않았다.
그러나 계곡의 버들강아지가
봄을 품고 왔다.

Effortless harmony with nature

Gathered and scattered, then gathered once more.
Mountain winds, gentle breezes, whispers of rivers,
the forsythia blooms at the foot of the hills,
their yellow murmurs bring tears to the heart,
yet no one has come.
But the willow catkins of the valley have arrived,
cradling the essence of spring.

겁외풍경의 미소 캔버스에 혼합물감, 91×116.8cm, 2022
Smiles of 'Landscapes beyond time (겁외풍경)' Mixed media on canvas, 91×116.8cm, 2022

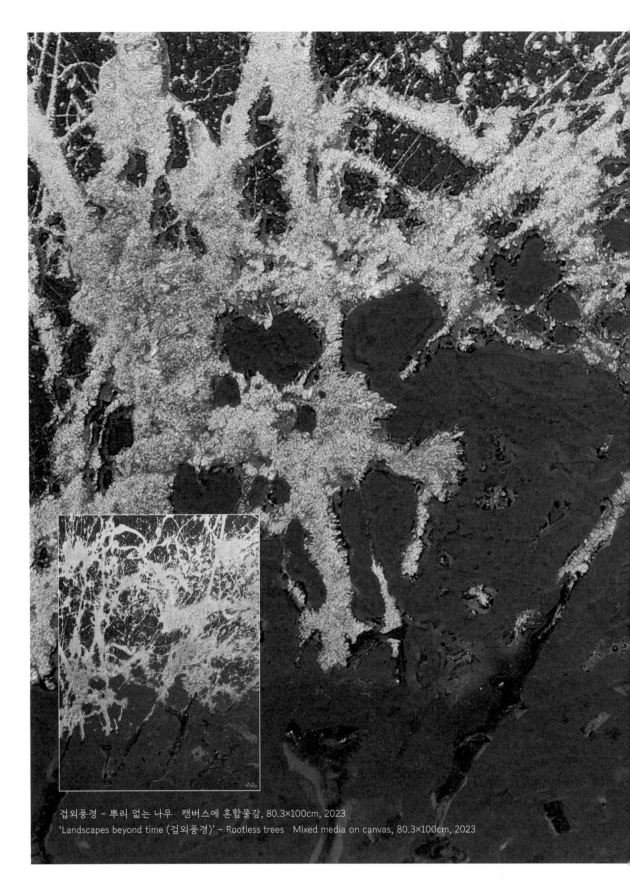

겁외풍경 - 뿌리 없는 나무 캔버스에 혼합물감, 80.3×100cm, 2023
'Landscapes beyond time (겁외풍경)' – Rootless trees   Mixed media on canvas, 80.3×100cm, 2023

얼음꽃

사람은 누구나 외롭고 고독하다.
그러나 이 외로움과 고독을 잘 품고 사는 사람은
눈 속에 피어난 얼음꽃처럼 가슴 서늘한 아름다움이 있다.
지독한 아픔도 견딜 줄 아는.

Ice flowers

Every soul knows the depths of loneliness.
Yet those who embrace this solitude,
like ice flowers blooming in the snow,
possess a beauty that chills the heart.
They are the ones who can endure,
the most profound pain.

60

노란 웅크림

세상 사람
누군들 아프지 않고 슬프지 않으랴.
누군들 외롭고 고독하지 않으랴.
다만 이 모든 것을 묵묵히 참고 견디는 사람과
그렇지 않은 사람이 있을 뿐이다.
성인군자도 아픈 건 아프고 슬픈 건 슬프다.
아무도 없는 산골짝 달빛 머금은 산유화
노란 웅크림이 애틋하다.

Yellow curls

Oh, to all the souls of the world,
who among you is untouched by pain or sorrow?
Who does not feel the weight of loneliness and solitude?
There are only those who endure quietly, and those who do not.
Even the sage feels pain, and sorrow weighs heavy.
In the empty mountain glade,
the moonlight cradles the mountain flower,
its yellow petals curl in tender yearning.

겹외풍경의 노래 캔버스에 혼합물감, 91×116.8cm, 2022
Hymns of 'Landscapes beyond time (겹외풍경)' Mixed media on canvas, 91×116.8cm, 2022

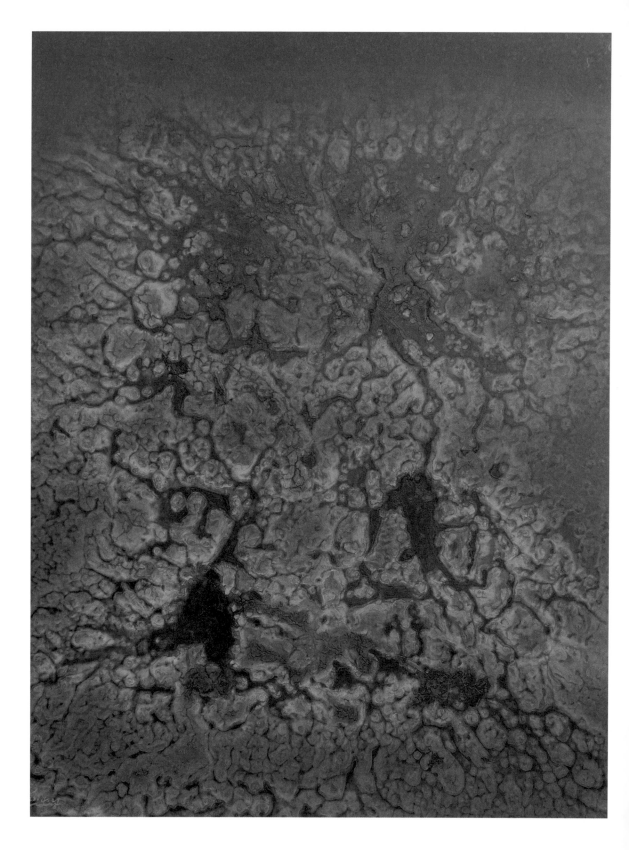

겁외풍경의 춤 캔버스에 혼합물감, 91×116.8cm, 2022
Dances of 'Landscapes beyond time (겁외풍경)' Mixed media on canvas, 91×116.8cm, 2022

아무런 이유 없이

만약 그대가
오늘 하루 눈물 날 만큼 외로웠다면
평소 무관심했던 사람들을 생각했을 것이요,
고독했다면 자신의 내면의 소리를 들었을 것이다.
그리고 쓸쓸했다면 아무런 이유 없이
세상 모든 것을 품었을 것이다.

Without any reason

If today you felt loneliness,
deep enough to bring tears,
you must have reflected on those you usually overlook.
In your solitude, you listened to the whispers of your soul,
and in your sadness, without reason,
you embraced the entirety of the world.

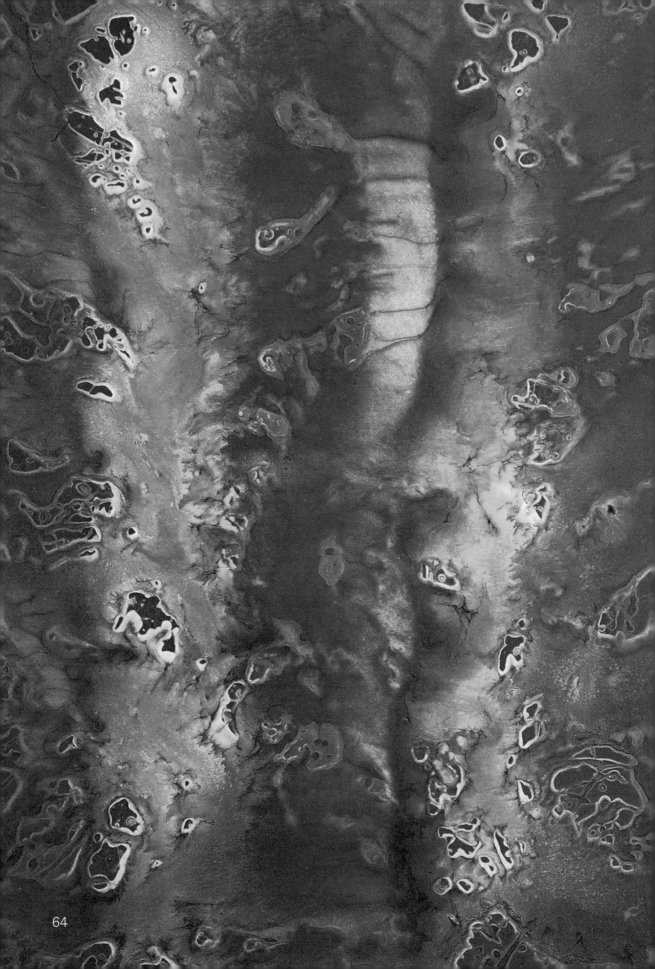

가진 채로 버려라

소인은 조금만 가져도 자랑 안 하면 못 살고
대인은 아무리 가져도 가졌다는 생각을 아니한다.
무소유란 아무것도 갖지 않는 것이 아니라
세상 모든 것을 다 가졌어도
내 것이란 어리석음에 빠지지 않는 것이다.
가진 채로 버려라, 이것이 진정한 무소유다.

Hold on, yet let go

Small minded people cannot live without boasting,
even with the slightest possession,
while great souls remain untouched by what they hold,
never claiming ownership, no matter how much they possess.
True non-attachment is not in having nothing,
but in embracing the world without falling into the folly of calling it 'mine.'
Hold on yet let go;
this is the essence of true non-attachment.

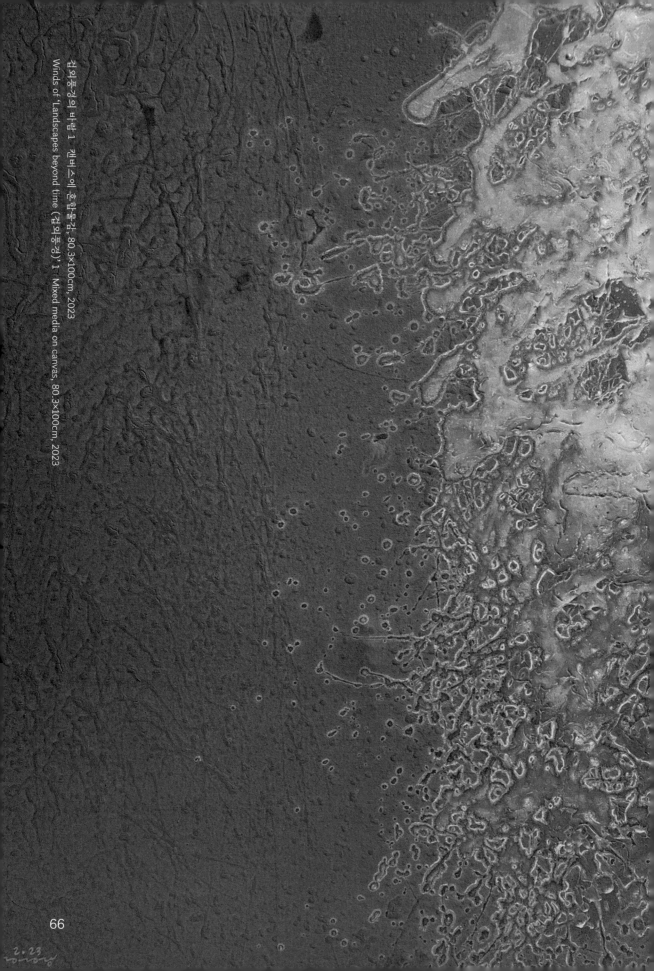

권외풍경의 바람 1 캔버스에 혼합물감, 80.3×100cm, 2023
Winds of 'Landscapes beyond time 〈권외풍경〉' 1 Mixed media on canvas, 80.3×100cm, 2023

그대가 빛이라면

어디서든 누구에게 빛을 받으려 하지 말고
스스로 빛이 되고자 하라.
인간은 누구나 무한대의 빛을 가지고 있다.
만약 그대가 빛이라면 쫓아다니며 뿌리려 하지 말고
고요히 앉아 번지게 하라.

If you are light

Do not seek the light from others,
but strive to become the light yourself.
Every soul carries within an infinite glow.
Say if you are light, do not go chasing after it,
but sit still, letting your brilliance spread.

넘어 넘어서 가라

인간이 만든 그 어떤 언어도
언어 그 자체가 진리인 경우는 없다.
말씀에 머물면 말씀의 노예가 되고
부처에 머물면 부처의 노예가 된다.
가라! 그 어떤 곳에도 머물지 말고
넘어 넘어서.

Transcend beyond

No language crafted by humankind is truth in itself.
To dwell in words is to become their slave,
to linger in the Buddha is to be bound by him.
Go forth! Do not stay anywhere,
but transcend beyond all bounds.

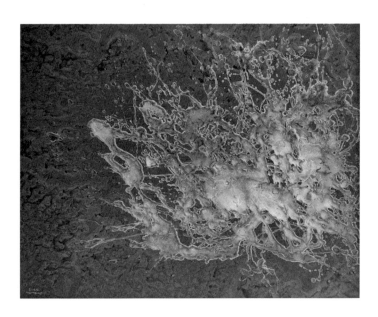

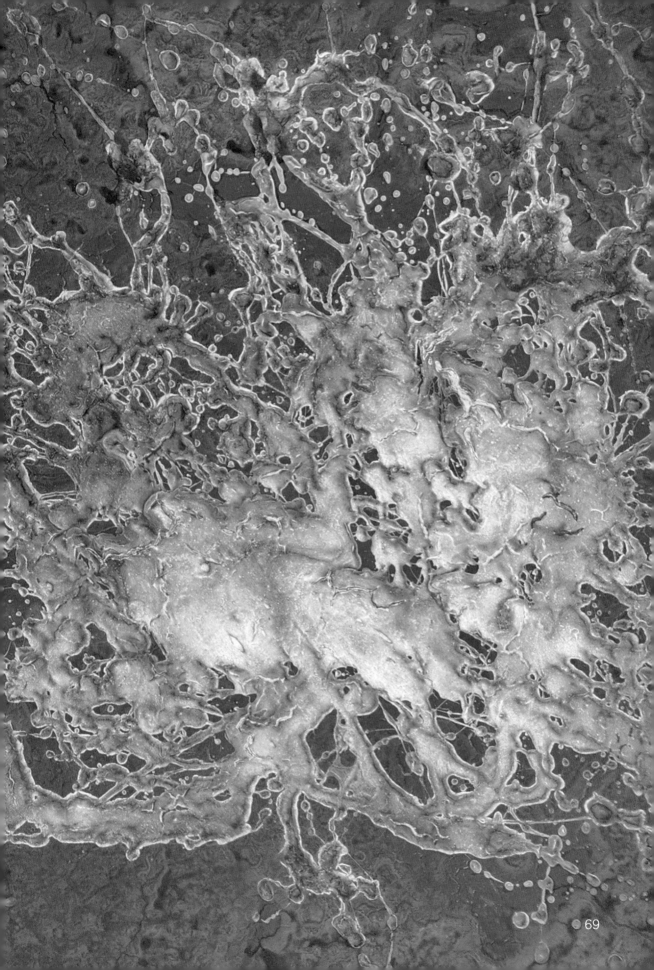

깨달음이란

물이 얼었다 녹았다 하는 것처럼
진리는 그대의 존재를 감싸고 때론 얼었다 녹았다
고요히 흐르다 거침없이 흐른다.
깨달음이란 자기를 버리고 만물과 함께
통쾌히 흐르는 자유를 말한다.

Enlightenment

Like water freezing and thawing,
truth envelops your being,
sometimes still, sometimes rushing,
flowing with serene ease.
Enlightenment speaks of casting off ourself,
flowing freely in joyful unity with all.

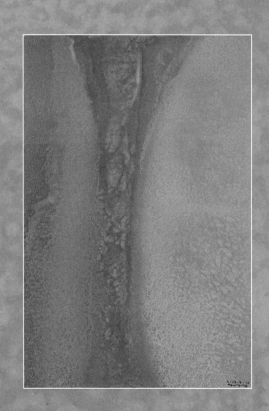

겹외풍경의 강 캔버스에 혼합물감, 8.3×116cm, 2022
Rivers of 'Landscapes beyond time (겹외풍경)' Mixed media on
canvas, 8.3×116cm, 2022

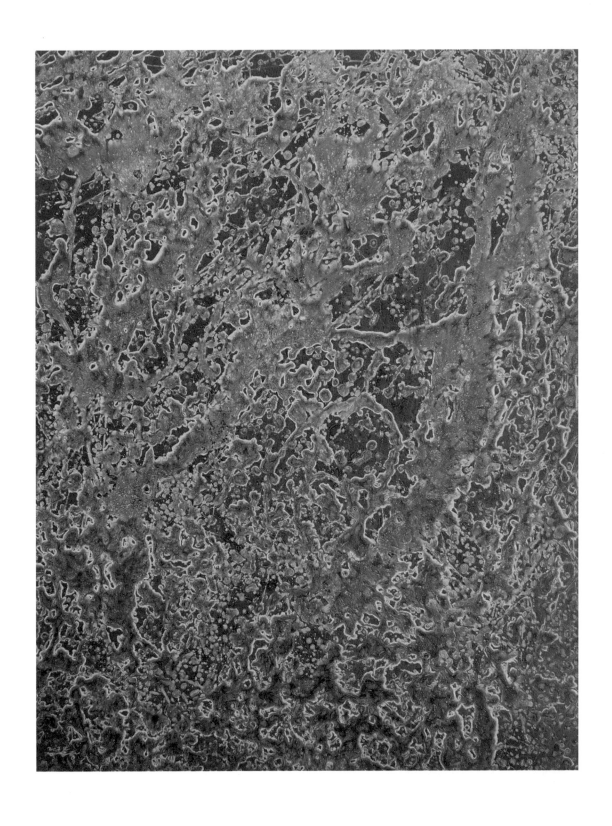

겁외풍경 − Jazz Blues 캔버스에 혼합물감, 72.7×90.9cm, 2022
'Landscapes beyond time (겁외풍경)' − Jazz Blues   Mixed media on canvas, 72.7×90.9cm, 2022

영롱한 이슬처럼

걸림 없이 산다는 것은
일체를 초월해 사는 것이 아니요,
순간을 전체로 사는 것이다.
매 순간 롱록 떨어지는 영롱한 이슬처럼
존재 그 자체를 단순히 놓고 노는 것이다.
자신을 부릴 줄 아는 사람은
천하를 부릴 줄 안다.

Dewdrops

Living without hindrance
is not to transcend all,
but to embrace each moment as the whole.
Like dewdrops that sparkle and fall,
it is to simply play with existence itself.
Those who master themselves,
hold power over the world.

참나

사람을 만나도 외롭고 안 만나도 외로운 것은
참나를 만나지 못했기 때문이요
사람을 만나도 공허하고 안 만나도 공허한 것은
참나로 살지 못하기 때문이다.

True self

To feel lonely in the company of others,
and lonely still in solitude,
is to have not yet found our true self.
To encounter emptiness in the company of others,
and absence still in solitude,
is to be unable to live in our true self.

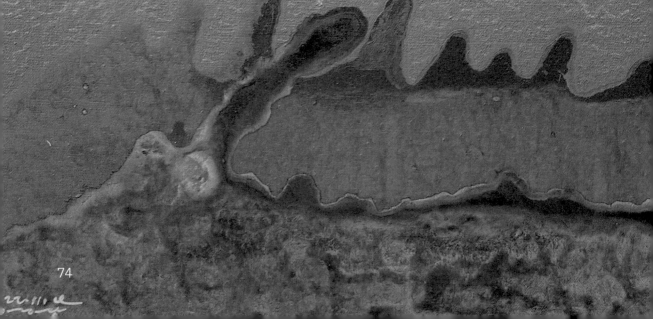

겁외풍경 – 태고의 숨 캔버스에 혼합물감, 91×65cm, 2022
'Landscapes beyond time (겁외풍경)' – Breath of the Primordial
Mixed media on canvas, 91×65cm, 2022

주인공의 삶

이리 가도 불행하고
저리 가도 불행한 사람이 있는가 하면
이리 가도 행복하고 저리 가도 행복한 사람이 있다.
전자는 자신의 욕망에 끄달리는 사람이고
후자는 그것으로부터 자유로운 사람이다.
어리석은 자는 어디를 가나 남의 종으로 살고
지혜로운 자는 어디를 가도 주인공으로 산다.

Protagonist

Some wander in sorrow, no matter the path they take,
while others find joy, whether here or there.
The former are led by their desires,
the latter live free from their chains.
The foolish serve as others' shadows wherever they roam,
while the wise walk as the protagonists of their own tale.

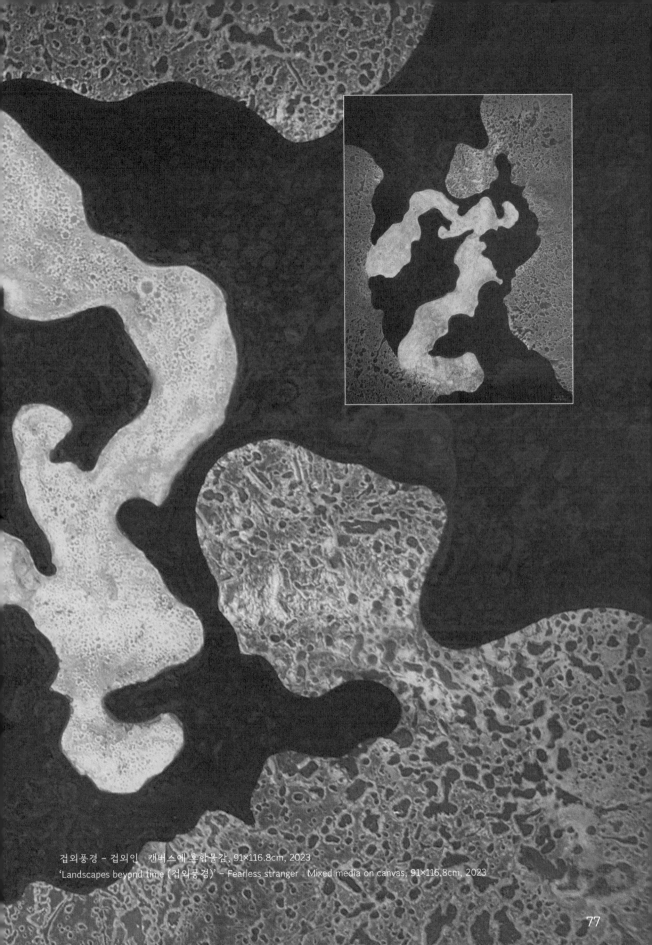

접외풍경 – 접외인 캔버스에 혼합물감, 91×116.8cm, 2023
'Landscapes beyond time (접외풍경)' – Fearless stranger Mixed media on canvas, 91×116.8cm, 2023

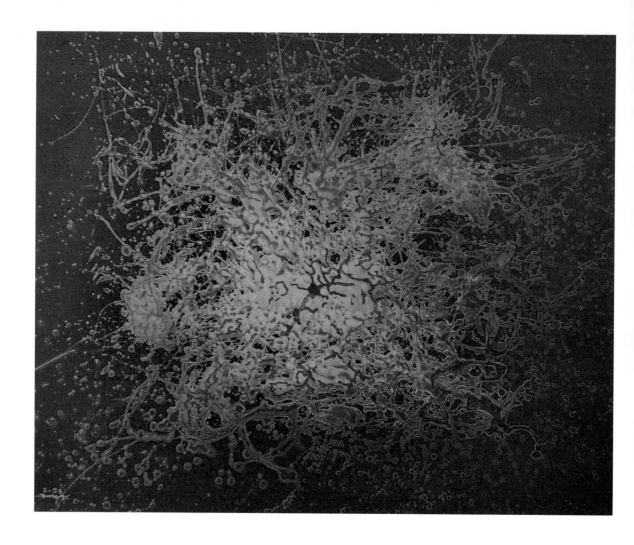

무소유

잔을 채울 땐 확실히 채우고 비울 땐 확실히 비우라.
무소유란 늘 빈 잔으로 있는 것이 아니라
채우고 비우는 데 걸림 없는 것을 말한다.

To possess nothing

Fill the cup with certainty, and when empty, let it be clear.
To possess nothing is not to hold an always-empty cup,
but to embrace the freedom of filling and pouring without restraint.

격외풍경 – 오케스트라 캔버스에 혼합물감, 100×80.3cm, 2022
'Landscapes beyond time (격외풍경)' – Orchestra Mixed media
on canvas, 100×80.3cm, 2022

붓을 던지니 새가 난다.
한 소리에 하늘이 깬다.
빈 마음으로 세상을 보니
천하가 내 밥상이다.

With a toss of the brush, a bird takes flight;
at that single sound, the sky awakens.
With an empty heart, I behold the world,
and the universe becomes my feast.

선승의 눈 – 관(觀) 화선지에 먹, 21×34cm, 2007
Eyes of the Zen master – Contemplation Ink on rice paper, 21×34cm, 2007

생명의 축제 – 적(寂) 화선지에 혼합물감, 280×110cm, 2001
Festival of life – Silence (寂)　Mixed media on rice paper, 280×110cm, 2001

지금 즉 영원

인생의 목표를
지금 살아 있는 그 순간에 두라.
순간이 영원이 되게 하라.
지금 행복하지 않으면
언제 행복할 수 있으랴.

Let each moment be eternal

Set the aim of our lives
in this very moment you breathe.
Let each moment become eternity.
If you are not happy now,
when will happiness find you?

진정한 예술

여기 있으면서 저기를 생각하고
저기 있으면서 여기를 생각하는 사람은
어디를 가도 불행하고,
여기서는 여기를 살고 저기서는 저기를 살면
어디를 가도 행복하다.
삶은 존재 그 자체를 놓고 노는 것.
진정한 예술은 그때그때 노는 것이다.

True art

Those who dwell here while thinking of there,
and there while anchored here,
will find sorrow wherever they go.
But to live fully in this place and that,
brings joy no matter the path.
Life is a dance with existence itself,
and true art is playing in each moment.

생명의 축제 – 환(歡) 화선지에 혼합물감, 280×110cm, 2001
Festival of life – Joy (歡) Mixed media on rice paper, 280×110cm, 2001

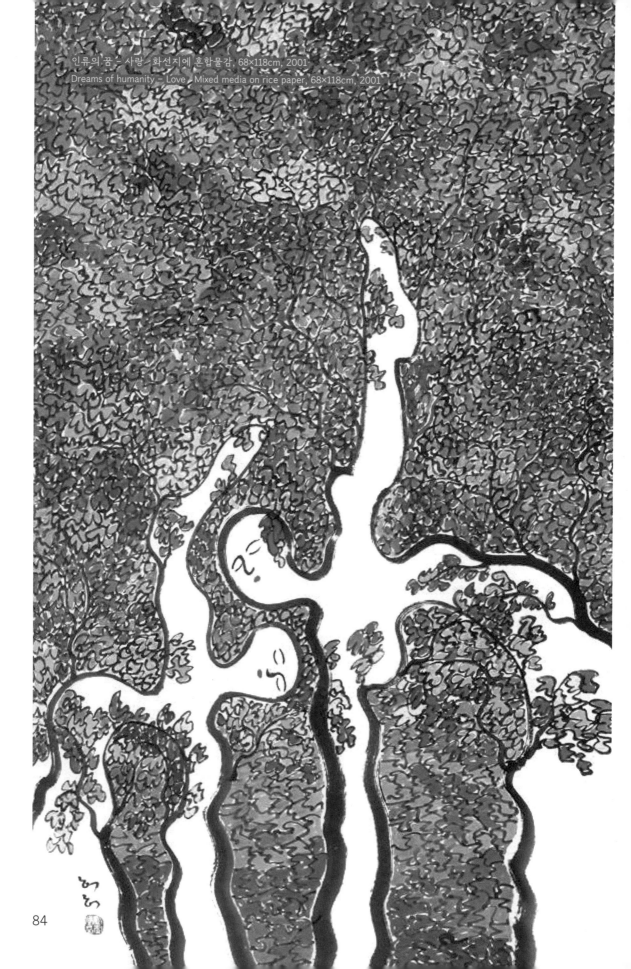

인류의 꿈 – 사랑 · 화선지에 혼합물감, 68×118cm, 2001
Dreams of humanity – Love · Mixed media on rice paper, 68×118cm, 2001

84

고정관념을 버려라

창조적인 사람은 늘 새로운 것에 대한 설렘이 있다.
누구나 이미 아는 것은 설렘이 없다.
사람을 만나도 설렘이 없는 것은
이미 상대를 알고 있다는 생각 때문이다.
모르는 것은 항상 신비롭다.

그대가 상대를 안다고 생각할 때 모든 신비는 사라진다.
상대를 안다고 하는 순간 그대는 상대를 만나는 것이 아니라
자신의 고정관념을 만날 뿐이다.

모든 아름다움은 상상 밖에 있다.
아는 길은 편안하지만 더 이상 신비로움이 없다.
창조적인 사람은 아는 길을 가지 않고 모르는 길을 간다.

Letting go of fixed notions

The creative soul is forever tinged with excitement for the new.
What is already known holds no thrill.
When meeting another, if there's no spark,
it's the thought of familiarity that dulls the heart.

The unknown remains eternally mysterious.
When you believe you know another, all wonder fades.
In claiming to understand, you meet not the other,
but merely your own fixed notions.

All beauty lies beyond the realm of imagination.
The well-trodden path feels safe, yet lacks the magic.
A creative spirit shuns the familiar road,
choosing instead to wander into the unknown.

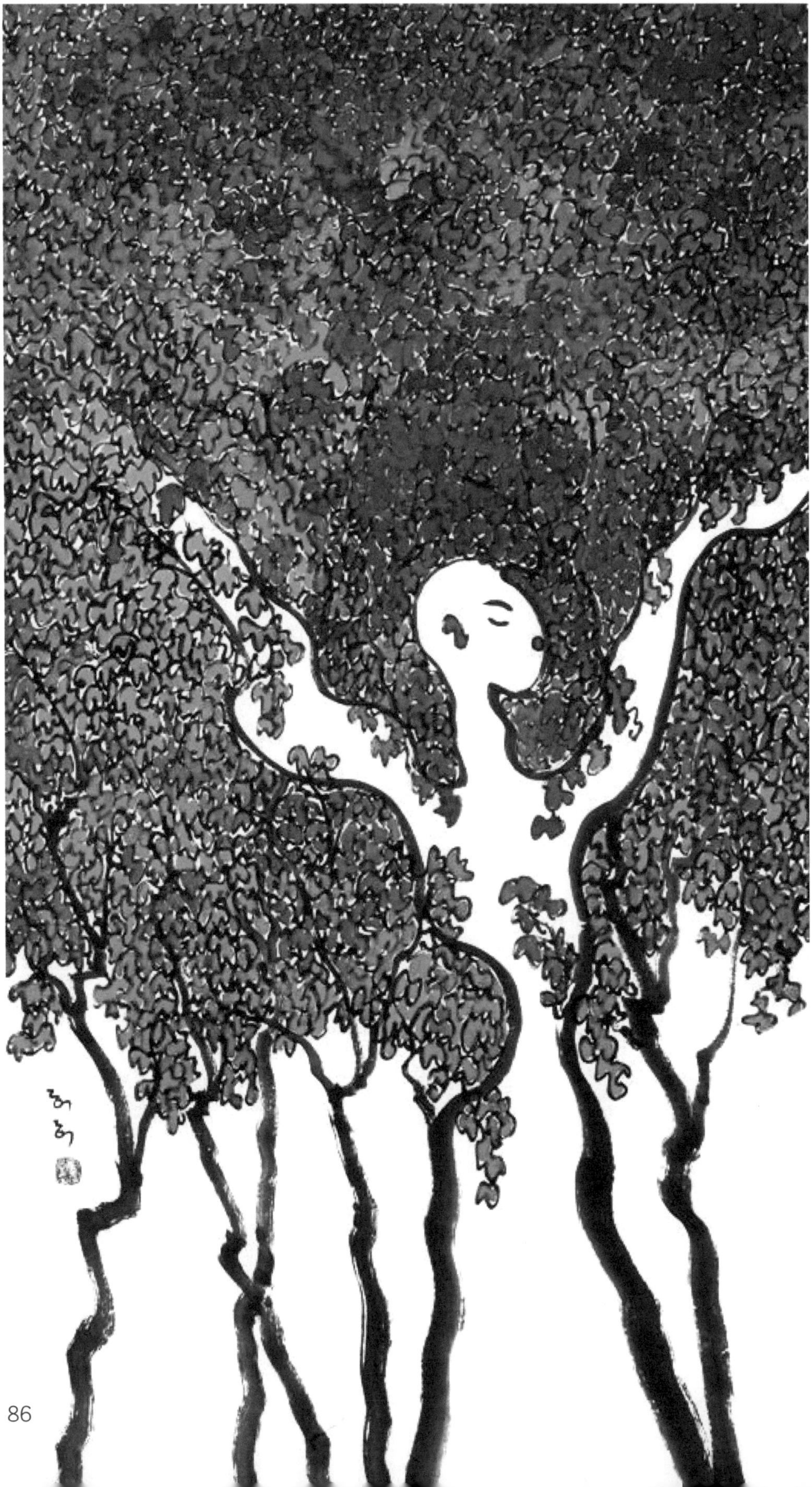

인류의 꿈 – 자유 화선지에 혼합물감, 68×118cm, 2001

Dreams of humanity – Freedom Mixed media on rice paper, 68×118cm, 2001

무슨 일이든

사람들은 철학이나 종교는 괜히 심오하거나
심오해야 된다고 생각한다.
때문에 평생 철학을 하고 종교를 믿어도 시원하지가 않다.
진리는 단순하다. 있는 그대로다.
무슨 일이든 노는 마음으로 하면 일 자체가 즐겁다.
도대체 세상 그 무엇이 놀지 않고 즐거울 수 있으랴!
철학도 종교도 즐거워야 한다.

Any task

People often believe that philosophy and religion must be profound,
leading to a lifetime of seeking without satisfaction.
Yet truth is simple, just as it is.
When approached with a playful heart,
any task becomes a joy.
What in this world can bring delight without play?
Both philosophy and faith should be sources of joy.

인간의 양심

불의를 보면 분노할 줄 알고 정의를 보면 기뻐하는 것이 참된 인간의 모습이다.
인간 양심을 저버린 그 어떤 철학이나 종교도 세상을 이롭게 하지 못한다.
아무리 많은 지식을 쌓아도 양심이 병든 자는 세상을 해롭게 하고
아무것을 몰라도 양심이 살아 있는 자는 세상을 이롭게 한다.
진실한 양심의 세계에는 두려움이 없다. 두려움은 오직 거짓의 세계에만 존재한다.
진리에 눈 뜬 자는 세상 그 어떤 불의에도 굴하지 않는다.

Human conscience

To see injustice and feel true anger,
to witness righteousness and rejoice;
this is the essence of a true human being.
No philosophy or faith that forsakes the human conscience
can ever benefit the world.
No matter how much knowledge one accumulates,
a conscience in decay harms the earth,
while one who knows nothing yet possesses a vibrant heart,
brings goodness to the world.
In the realm of a genuine conscience, fear holds no power;
it exists only in the domain of falsehood.
Those awakened to truth stand firm against all injustice.

인류의 꿈 – 공생 화선지에 수채화물감, 47×83cm, 2001
Dreams of humanity – Coexistence Watercolor on ricepaper, 47×83cm, 2001

진리는

진리는 인간적이지도 도덕적이지도 않다.
진리는 아주 냉철하고 비정하다.
그러나 이 뜻을 명확히 아는 자는
더없이 인간적이다.

The truth

Truth is neither humane nor moral;
it is cruel and unyielding.
Yet those who grasp this meaning
are profoundly humane in their essence.

인류의 꿈 – 평화 화선지에 동양화물감, 72×100cm, 2002
Dreams of humanity – Peace Ink on rice paper, Oriental painting pigments, 72×100cm, 2002

아이폰 소녀　화선지에 혼합물감, 67×91cm, 2014, 아마존 여행 중
Iphone girl　Mixed media on rice paper, 67×91cm, 2014, During a trip in the Amazon

이름

이름은 하나의 그리움이다.
좋은 이름은 설사 거기에 아무것이 없다 해도
절대 실망하거나 후회하지 않는다.
단지 그 이름만으로도 내 안에 또 다른 세계를 펼쳐 놓는다.
아마존 아마존은 그 이름만으로도
나를 충분히 행복하게 했다.

A name

A name is a longing in itself.
A beautiful name, even in emptiness,
never brings disappointment or regret.
With just that name, it unfolds another world within me.
'Amazon' – just the sound of it
has brought me boundless joy.

그대 지금 길이 없다면
고요히 앉아 자신을 보라.
모든 길은 자신을 통한다.

If no path is to be found before you now,
sit quietly and look within.
Every road begins with the self.

바람의 기억 – 순례자 1 화선지에 혼합물감, 65×72cm, 2014
Memories of the wind – Pilgrim 1 Mixed media on rice paper, 65×72cm, 2014

자유롭다는 것은 모든 것을 벗어나 홀로 있는 것이 아니라
모든 것을 품고도 걸림 없는 것을 말한다.

To be free is not to stand apart from all,
but to embrace everything without hindrance.

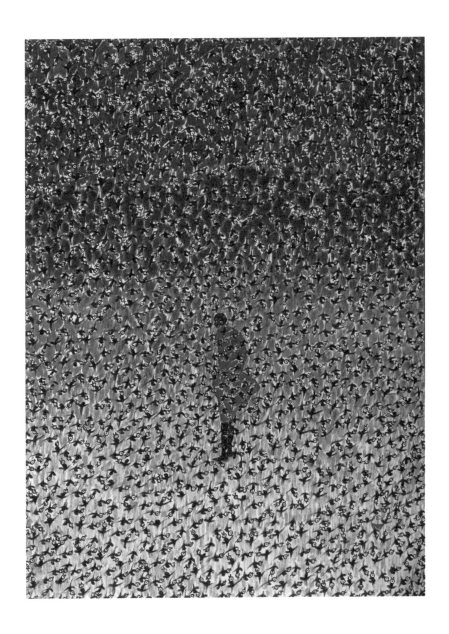

바람의 기억 – 사유. 화선지에 혼합물감, 67×90cm, 2014
Memories of the wind – Contemplation. Mixed media on rice paper, 67×90cm, 2014

건강한 사회

가장 좋은 세상은 종교 없는 세상이요,
가장 건강한 사회는 병원 없는 사회다.
종교가 많다는 것은 그만큼 세상이 타락했다는 증거요,
병원이 많다는 것은 그만큼 사회가 병들었다는 증거다.

A healthy society

The greatest of worlds is one without religion,
and the healthiest society is one without hospitals.
The abundance of religions reflects the world's decay,
while the abundance of hospitals reflects a society in sickness.

바람의 기억 – 해를 삼키는 타조　화선지에 혼합물감, 65.2×73cm, 2014
Memories of the wind – Ostrich swallowing the sun　Mixed media on rice paper, 65.2×73cm, 2014

비도덕

진리는 도덕도 부도덕도 아니다.
누가 나무를 보고 도덕이다 부도덕이다 시비하던가?
일체 만물은 모두 비도덕이다.
자연은 있는 그대로 진리이다.

Beyond morality

Truth is neither moral nor immoral.
Who debates if a tree is moral or not?
All things exist beyond morality.
Nature, in its essence, is truth unveiled.

바람의 기억 – 달 구경하는 사람 화선지에 혼합물감, 67×90cm, 2014
Memories of the wind – Moongazing Mixed media on rice paper, 67×90cm, 2014

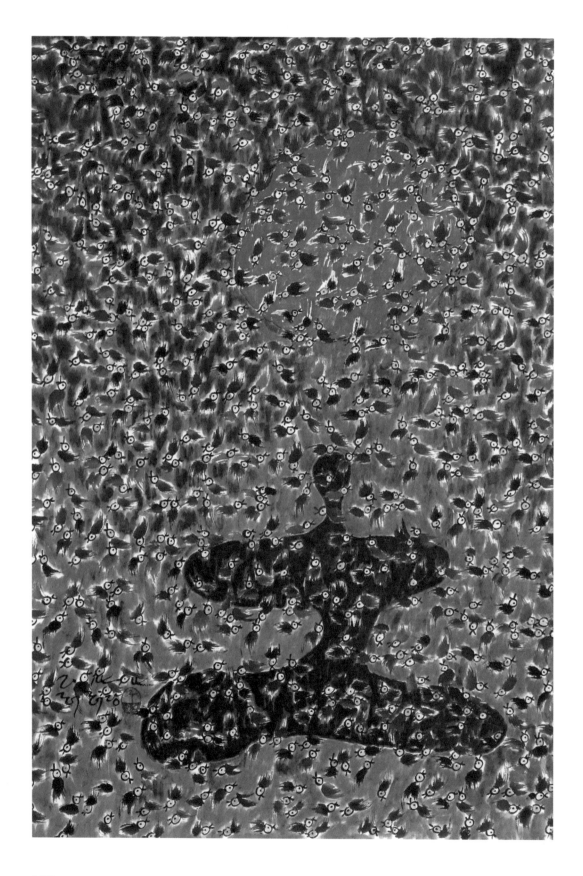

100

큰 스승

아무런 경계 없이 홀로 있으면
쓸쓸한 사막이어도 좋고 황량한 벌판이어도 좋다.
자신과의 정직한 대화, 이보다 더 큰 스승은 없다.
자신을 바로 보는 것,
이보다 큰 스승이 어디 있으랴.

A great master

To be alone without boundaries,
whether in a lonely desert or a barren field,
is to find a profound solitude.
There is no greater teacher than honest dialogue with oneself.
To see oneself clearly,
what greater guide could there be?

바람의 기억 – 옛 사람   화선지에 수채화물감, 71×90cm, 2013
Memories of the wind – Ancient soul   Watercolor on rice paper, 71×90cm, 2013

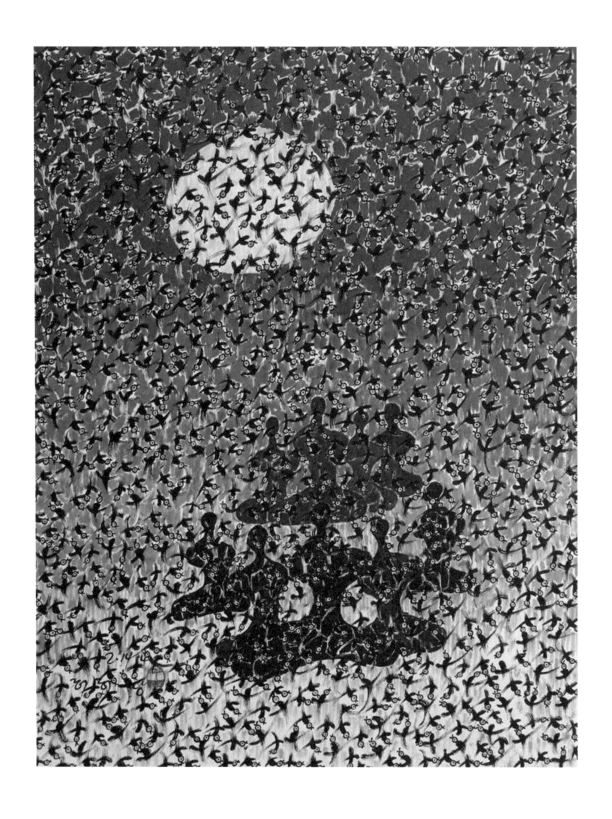

바람의 기억 – 선정　화선지에 먹 수채화물감, 71×90cm, 2013
Memories of the wind – Zen meditation　Watercolor and ink on rice paper, 71×90cm, 2013

깨를 털듯이

깨를 쏟듯 탈탈 쏟아라.
그대 가슴의 슬픔을 도리깨로 마구 쳐라.
그대 가슴의 절망을 그리고 일어나라,
존재의 기쁨으로.

깨를 털듯 탈탈 털어라.
그대 존재의 빈 껍질을 도리깨로 마구 쳐라.
그대 존재의 허상을 그리고 일어나라,
고요한 빛으로.

Like grains spilled

Like grains spilled, let your spirit pour forth.
With a flail, strike at the sorrow of your heart.
Rise from despair, embracing the joy of existence.

Shake off like husks,
beat away the empty shell of your being.
Rise from the illusion of self, transformed by tranquil light.

바람의 기억 – 도반(道伴) 화선지에 혼합물감, 65.2×73cm, 2014
Memories of the wind – Fellow traveler on the path (道伴) Mixed media on rice paper, 65.2×73cm, 2014

완전한 몰입

세상이 아무리 바빠도
빈둥거릴 줄 아는 자는 축복받은 사람이다.
묘하게도 인류의 지혜는 이 빈둥거림 속에서 나온다.
온전한 빈둥거림은 완전한 몰입이다.

The perfect immersion

No matter how busy we find the world to be,
those who know how to idle are truly blessed.
Strangely, the wisdom of humanity emerges from this idleness.
True idleness is perfect immersion.

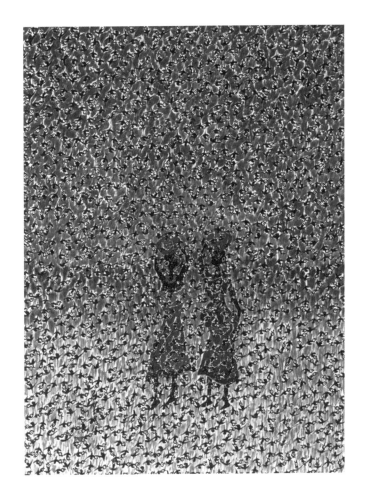

바람의 기억 - 거룩한 삶 화선지에 혼합물감, 65×90cm, 2014
Memories of the wind - Holy life Mixed media on rice paper, 65×90cm, 2014

속고 속이는 것

세상은 너를 속이지 않는다.
너 또한 세상을 속일 수 없다.
속고 속이는 것은
자신 이외 아무것도 없다.

Deception

The world does not deceive you,
nor can you deceive the world.
Deception exists only within yourself,
and nothing else.

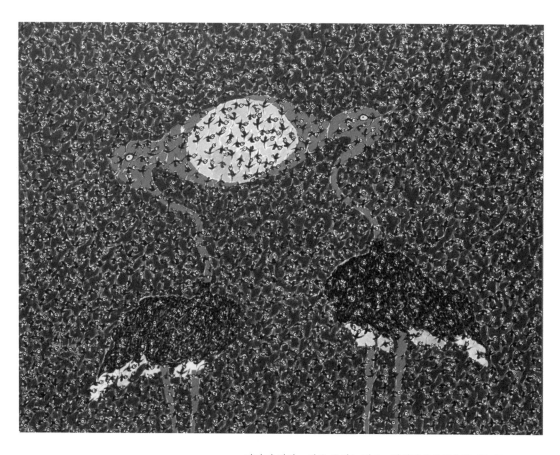

바람의 기억 – 달을 옮기는 타조 화선지에 혼합물감, 72×65cm, 2014
Memories of the wind – Ostrich moving the moon   Mixed media on rice paper, 72×65cm, 2014

예술가의 길

생판 모르는 길, 예술가는 모름지기 생판 모르는 길을 가야 한다.
그래야 비로소 자유로울 수 있다. 그래야 비로소 예술가라 할 수 있다.
화가는 그림을 파는 것이 아니라 자신의 삶과 영혼을 전하는 것이다.
따라서 멋진 예술가는 타인의 삶과 영혼을 눈뜨게 해 준다.

The path of an artist

On the path of the utterly unknown, the artist must tread without fear.
Only then can true freedom arise; only then can one truly be called an artist.
The painter does not sell mere paintings, but conveys the essence of life and soul.
Thus, a great artist awakens the lives and spirits of others.

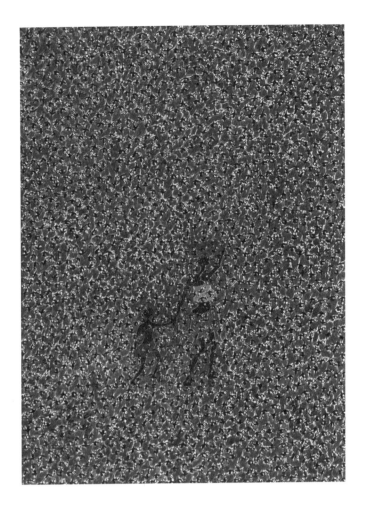

바람의 기억 – 행복한 모자 화선지에 혼합물감, 65.2×73cm, 2014
Memories of the wind – A happy mother and son Mixed media on rice paper, 65.2×73cm, 2014

우리 모두

죽어 가면서도 삶을 노래하는 사람이 있다.
아마도 그 노래는 이 세상 모든 것이 행복하라는 것일 게다.
나도 당신도 이 노래를 멋지게 부르다 갈 수 있기를.

Us all

There are those who sing of life even as they fade.
Perhaps their song is a wish for happiness for all that exists.
May both you and I sing this melody beautifully as we depart.

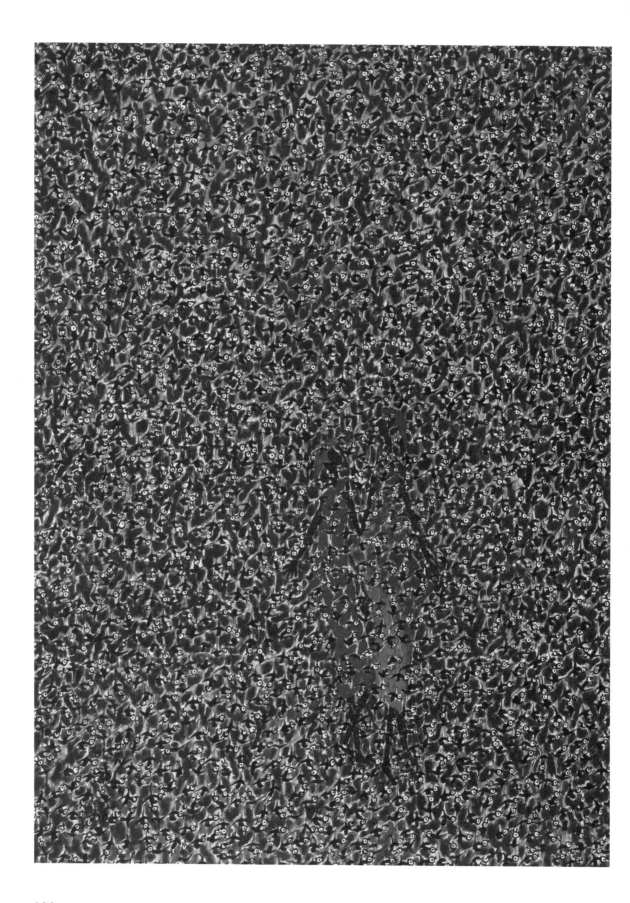

그대 어찌

세상은 가지는 것이 아니라 품는 것이다.
취하는 것이 아니라 담는 것이다.
세상은 있는 그대로 진실하여 정직한 사람에게 절로 안긴다.
그대 어찌 거짓된 마음으로 세상을 품으려 하는가?
가지려 하는가?

How you wander

The world is not for grasping, but for embracing.
It is not for taking, but for holding.
The universe finds its way
to those who possess a sincere heart.
How can one seek to embrace this world
with a heart tainted by deceit?

바람의 기억 – 자매의 사랑   화선지에 혼합물감, 67×90cm, 2014
Memories of the wind – Love of sisters   Mixed media on rice paper, 67×90cm, 2014

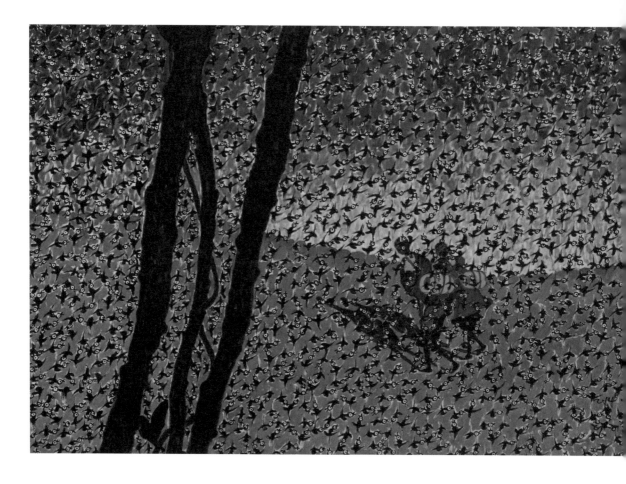

바람의 기억 – 귀가　화선지에 혼합물감, 73x65cm, 2014
Memories of the wind – Homecoming　Mixed media on rice paper,
73x65cm, 2014

혼의 울림

사람과 사람의 만남은 모름지기 혼의 울림이 있어야 한다.
혼의 울림이 있는 사람은 평생 한 번을 만나도 영원하다.
멀리 있어도 또렷하고 가까이 있어도 또렷하다.
그대 가슴에 울림이 있다면
눈을 감아도 보이고 귀를 닫아도 들린다.

Echos of our soul

A meeting of two souls must echo with depth,
for those who resonate remain eternal; time cannot sever.
Far yet clear, near yet bright.
If your heart vibrates, close your eyes,
their light still shines; their voice still calls.

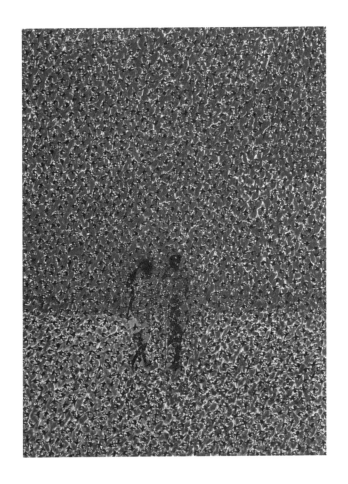

바람의 기억 – 휴식   화선지에 혼합물감, 65×72cm, 2014
Memories of the wind – Respite   Mixed media on rice paper, 65×72cm, 2014

아무리 아름다운 강산도

사람이 살면서
한 그루의 고목같이 기품 있게 늙는 것
이보다 멋진 일이 또 있을까?
아무리 아름다운 강산도
기품 있는 사람만 못하다.

No landscape's charm

To grow with grace, like an old tree's might,
Is there a beauty more pure and bright?
No landscape's charm, however grand,
can match the elegance of a noble hand.

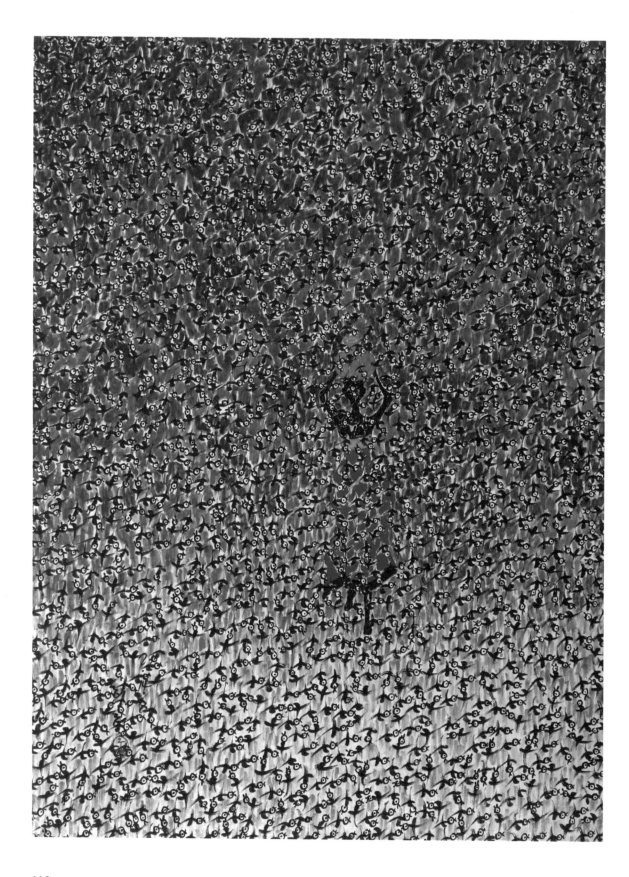

고요한 마음

배워서 아는 것은 유한하고 절로 아는 것은 무한하다.
인생은 모름지기 절로 아는 때에 비로소 자유로울 수 있다.

헐떡이는 마음은 채워도 채워도 부족함이 있고
고요한 마음은 비워도 비워도 부족함이 없다.
부족함이 없는 마음이라야 어디서든 자유롭다.

A tranquil heart

What we learn is finite, yet what we grasp within is endless,
Only in the knowing of the heart can life find freedom.

A restless heart, ever yearning, feels a constant lack,
While a tranquil heart, though emptied, knows no want.
It is the heart without need that finds freedom anywhere.

바람의 기억 – 마사이족 여인   화선지에 혼합물감, 67×90cm, 2014
Memories of the wind – A woman of the Maasai   Mixed media on rice paper, 67×90cm, 2014

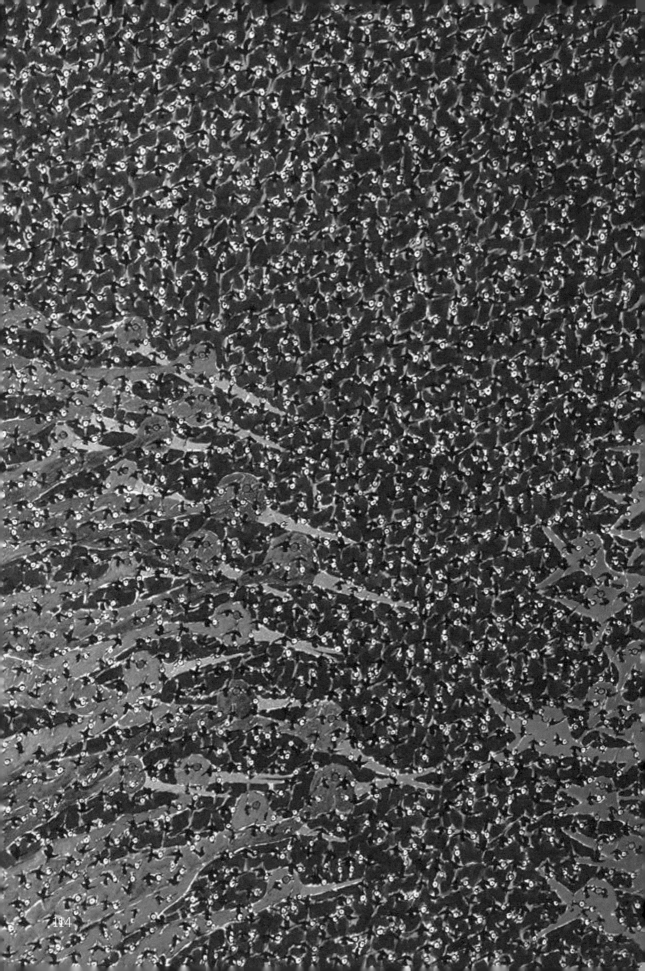

북두칠성과 세월호

새벽 달빛이 차다.
달무리 속 별 하나 어린 자식을 품고 있다.
지붕 위에 걸린 북두칠성 마지막 꼬리 별은 뒷산이 훔쳐 가고
여섯 개의 별이 남아 맥없이 반짝인다.
마치 사랑하는 가족을 잃은 슬픔인 양
세월호 유가족이 생각나는 밤이다.

The Big Dipper and the Sewol

The dawn moonlight is full and bright,
Within its halo, a star cradles a child.
The last tail star of the Big Dipper,
stolen away by the mountain's shadow,
leaving six stars to flicker weakly.
Tonight, like the sorrow of losing a beloved family,
the families of the Sewol victims come to mind.

바람의 기억 – 팽목항 화선지에 금분&혼합물감, 65.2×73cm, 2015, 4.19 추모작
Memories of the wind – Paengmok harbor Mixed media and gold leaf on rice paper,
65.2×73cm, 2015, 4.19 Tribute

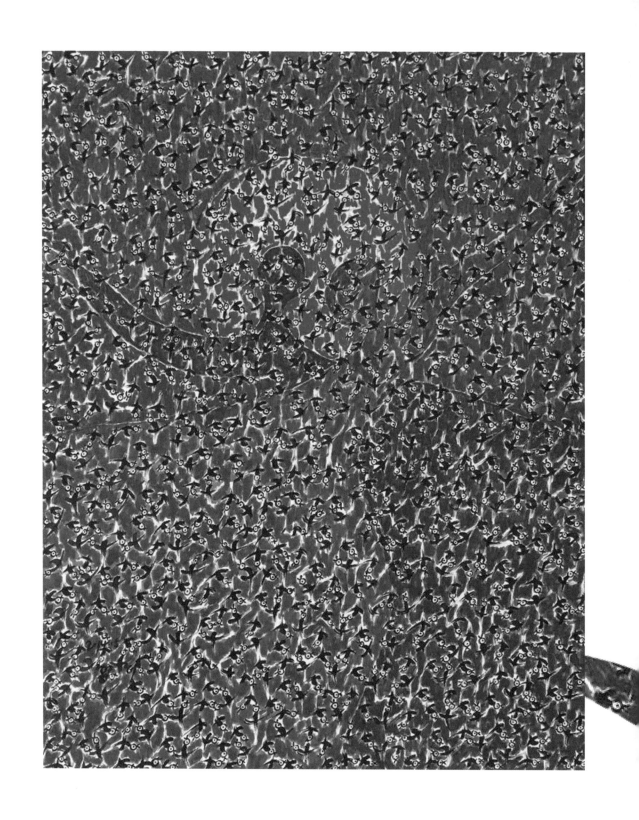

바람의 기억 – 천지창조 화선지에 혼합물감, 65.2×73cm, 2014
Memories of the wind – The creation Mixed media on rice paper, 65.2×73cm, 2014

무심히 부는 바람

지금 부는 바람은 천년 전에도 불었고
천년 후에도 불 것이다.
무심히 부는 바람에 과거 현재 미래가 없듯이
무심히 사는 사람은 과거 현재 미래가 없다.
오직 지금이 있을 뿐이다.

The indifferent breeze

The wind that breathes today has echoed a thousand years ago,
and shall blow a thousand years hence.
As the indifferent breeze knows not past, present, nor future,
So too does a life lived without care remain free from time.
where now is all that remains.

117

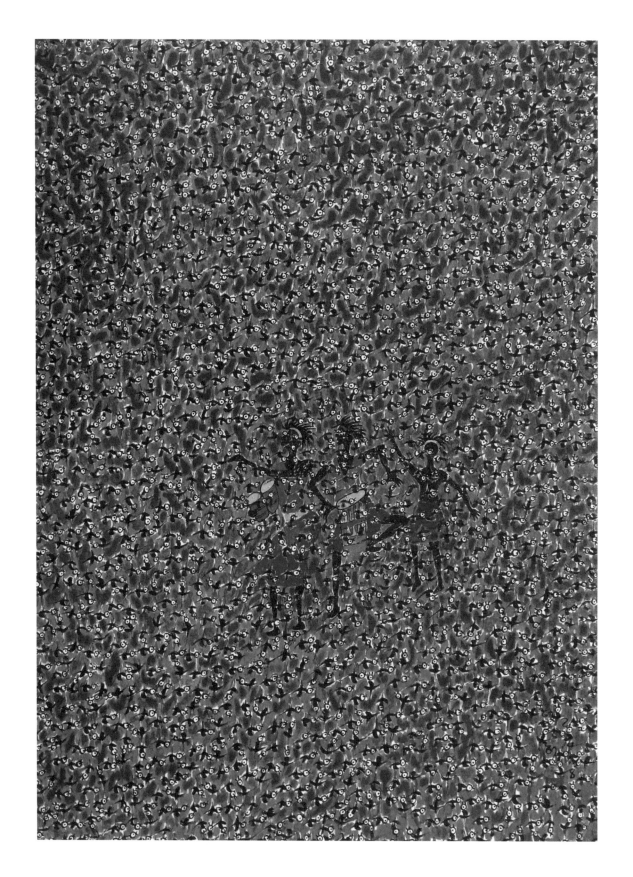

천진한 농담

그저 농담 조금 장난 조금.
인생을 이리 말하면 너무 허망할까?
하지만 내 살아 보니 인생은
장난 조금 농담 조금 그뿐이더라.
농담을 알면 진리가 보인다.
진리는 있는 그대로 농담하게 드러난다.

천진한 농담 속엔
온갖 신들이 웃음을 터트린다.

Innocent jests

Just a jest here, a playful tease there.
Is it too fleeting to speak of life this way?
Yet in my living, I've found it true:
Life is but a sprinkle of jest and play.
In laughter, the truth begins to shine;
The truth reveals itself, a jest divine.

Within innocent jests, all gods delight,
bursting forth in joyous laughter's light.

바람의 기억 – 마사이족의 축제　화선지에 혼합물감, 67×90cm, 2014
Memories of the wind – Festival of the Maasai　Mixed media on rice paper, 67×90cm, 2014

왼발은 뜨고 오른발은 닿네

내 지난날을 되돌아보니
아무런 할 일 없이 오고 갔었네.
지금 길을 멈추고 생각해 보니
온 일도 없고 간 일도 없네.

몸을 굽혀 앞을 보니
왼발은 뜨고 오른발은 닿네.

My left foot hovers, while the right stays grounded

As I reflect on days gone by,
I see I came and went without a purpose.
Now I pause and ponder my path,
finding neither deeds done nor paths crossed.

Bending low to gaze ahead,
my left foot hovers, while the right stays grounded.

반가사유상 한지에 먹, 22×33cm, 2018
The Pensive Bodhisattva Ink on hanji, 22×33cm, 2018

지금 이 순간

세상 사람 모두가 그대 곁을 떠나도
그리 슬픈 일이 아니다.
참으로 그대가 슬퍼해야 할 일은
지금 이 순간
그대 자신을 모르고 있다는 것.

At this moment

If the world should leave your side,
it's not such a sorrowful plight.
The true reason for your tears should be,
at this very moment,
when you do not know yourself.

겹외풍경 – 활구진언(살아 있는 진리의 말) 캔버스에 혼합물감, 130.3×162.2cm, 2024
'Landscapes beyond time (겹외풍경)' – 활구진언 (The living Word of Truth)
Mixed media on canvas, 130.3×162.2cm, 2024

겁외풍경의 바다 캔버스에 혼합물감, 91×65.1cm, 2023
Oceans of 'Landscapes beyond time (겁외풍경)' Mixed media on canvas, 91×65.1cm, 2023

인생은 서핑이다

세상이 아무리 힘들고 어려워도
자신을 바로 보는 사람은 마치 험한 파도를 타고 놀듯이
자신의 삶을 즐길 줄 안다.

살아간다는 건 고해의 바다에 빠지지 않고 슬기롭게 노는 것
서핑을 할 줄 아는 사람은 거친 파도일수록
더욱더 신난다.

Life is surfing

No matter how tough the world may be,
those who see themselves with clarity
can ride the tumultuous waves of life,
finding joy in the stormy sea.

To live is to dance wisely upon
the waters of despair, avoiding the deep;
For those who know the art of surfing
find thrill in every crashing wave.

124

홀연히 떠나는 자

그대를 비난하는 사람도 있고
칭찬하는 사람도 있다.
그러나 그 어떤 비난과 칭찬에도 머물지 마라.
무엇이든 홀연히 떠나는 자에겐
늘 새로운 세계가 기다리고 있다.

Those who let go with grace

There are those who cast blame,
and others who sing your praise.
Yet do not linger in either shadow;
For to those who let go with grace,
a new world always awaits.

겹외풍경 – 황홀경 캔버스에 혼합물감, 91×116.8cm, 2022
'Landscapes beyond time (겹외풍경)' – Ecstasy Mixed media on canvas, 91×116.8cm, 2022

겁외풍경의 바람 3 캔버스에 혼합물감, 65.2×91cm, 2022
Winds of 'Landscapes beyond time (겁외풍경)' 3   Mixed media on canvas, 65.2×91cm, 2022

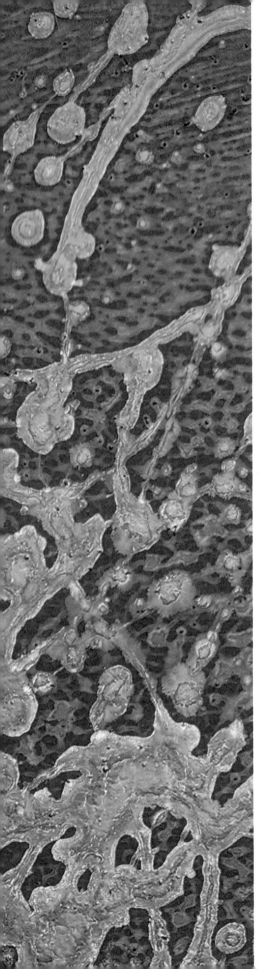

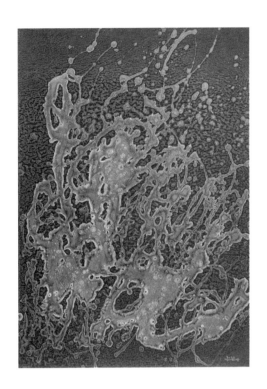

머물지 마라, 그 어떤 것에도

모든 것은 있다 없다 하는 거다.
돈도 사랑도 이별도
오늘 있다고 영원히 있는 것이 아니요,
오늘 없다고 영원히 없는 것도 아니다.
머물지 마라, 그 어떤 것에도.

Do not linger, in anything at all.

All things are but whispers of being and not.
Wealth, love, and parting;
None are forever present, nor eternally lost.
What is here today may fade,
What is gone may return.
Do not linger, in anything at all.

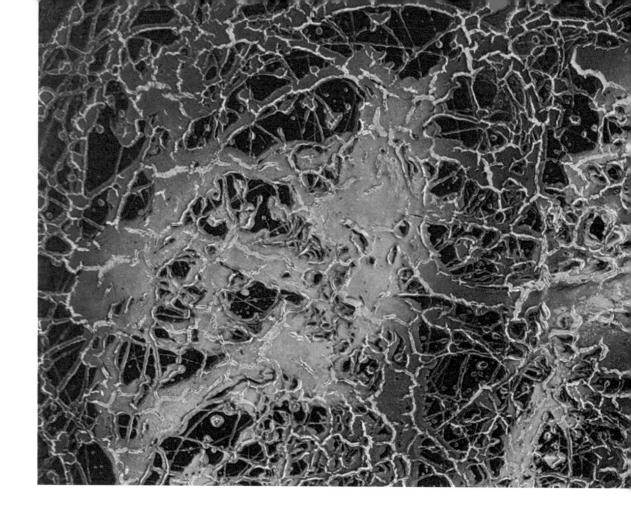

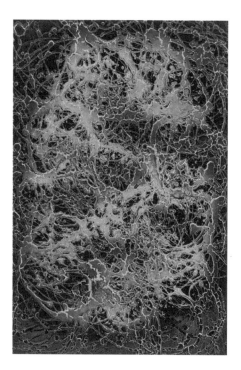

겁외풍경 – 깨어 있는 상처 캔버스에 혼합물감, 80.3×116.8cm, 2023
'Landscapes beyond time (겁외풍경)' – Awakened Wounds
Mixed media on canvas, 80.3×116.8cm, 2023

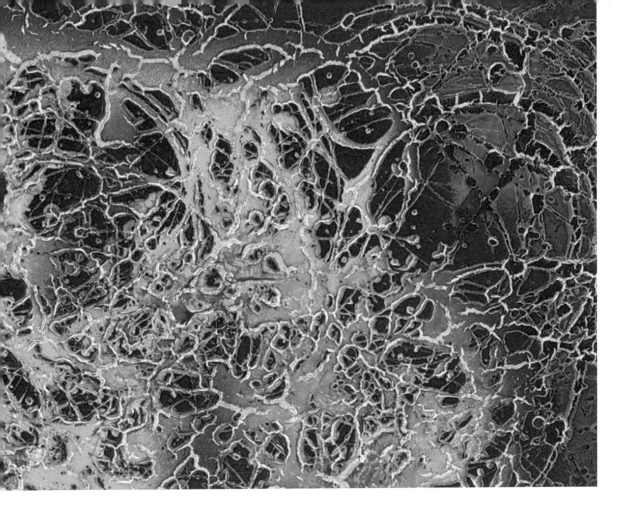

상처받지 않으려면

무엇이든 하나를 놓고 전부라 생각하지 마라.
그것이 무엇이든, 사랑 이별 혹은 진리일지라도
그것을 전부라고 생각하는 순간
반드시 마음에 상처를 받는다.

To leave no scars

Do not mistake one thing for the whole.
Whether love, loss, or truth.
The moment you believe it to be all,
your heart will surely bear the scars.

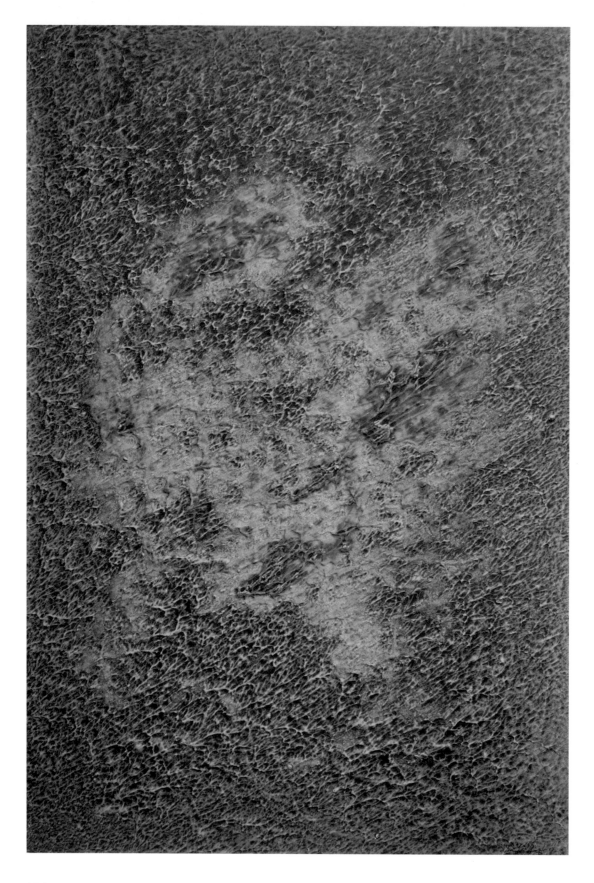

감동이란

누가 말한다, 어디 가면 멋진 소나무가 있다고.
사람들이 쫓아간다, 멋진 소나무를 보기 위해.
그러나 막상 그 소나무 앞에 선 사람들은
아무런 감동 없이 돌아선다. 그리고 다시 쫓아간다.
감동이란 찾아가는 것이 아니라 찾아오는 것이다.
무심히 길을 걷다 문득 내 앞에 나타난 한 그루의 소나무,
얼마나 멋지고 아름다운가?

True awe

One speaks of a majestic pine that waits ahead.
People rush forth, eager to behold its grace.
Yet standing before the tree,
they turn away, untouched, and hurry off once more.
For true awe does not come from pursuit;
It arrives unexpectedly, like a solitary pine
that appears along a wandering path.
How splendid and beautiful it truly is.

겁외풍경 – 활구풍언(살아 있는 바람의 말) 캔버스에 혼합물감, 80.3×116.8cm, 2024
'Landscapes beyond time (겁외풍경)' – 활구풍언 (The living Word of Wind)
Mixed media on canvas, 80.3×116.8cm, 2024

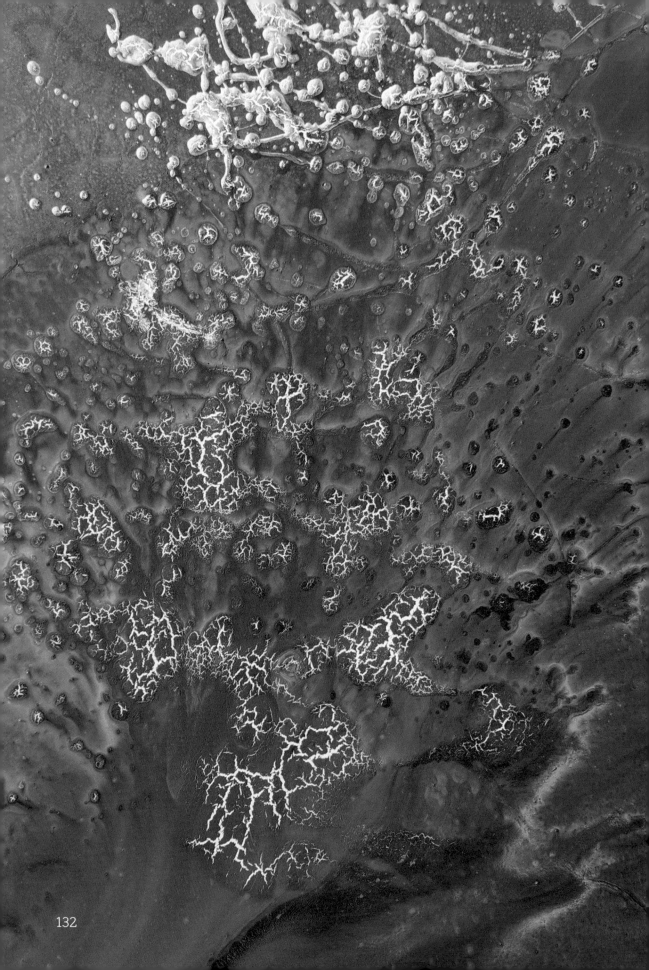

진실한 마음

사람이 가장 아름다울 때는
진실한 마음이 전해지는 눈빛과 가슴
그 순간을 마주할 때이다.

The true heart

The most beautiful moment of a person
is when their true heart shines through their eyes,
and the soul is met with open arms.

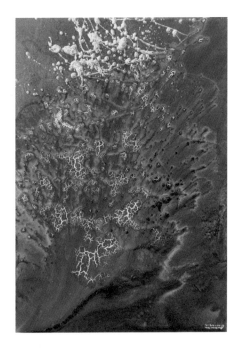

겁외풍경 – 니체의 산문 캔버스에 혼합물감, 72.7×100cm, 2022
'Landscapes beyond time (겁외풍경)' – Nietzsche's prose
Mixed media on canvas, 72.7×100cm, 2022

깨달음

날마다 태양은 떠오른다.
태양이 무엇을 책임지기 위해
또는 의무이기 때문에 떠오르는 것은 아니다.
그러나 만물은 제각기 필요한 만큼
태양을 의지하며 살아간다.
깨달음도 이와 같다.

Awakening of the mind

Each day, the sun rises anew,
not to fulfill a duty or bear a weight.
Yet all things, in their own need,
depend on its light to thrive.
Awakening of our minds, too, is much the same.

겹외풍경 – 녹색 태양 캔버스에 혼합물감, 80.3×116cm, 2022
'Landscapes beyond time (겹외풍경)' – Emerald sun   Mixed media on canvas, 80.3×116cm, 2022

겹의풍경 – 존재의 꽃 캔버스에 혼합물감, 80.3×100cm, 2023
'Landscapes beyond time (겹의풍경)' – Flowers of existence Mixed media on canvas, 80.3×100cm, 2023

존재의 꽃

소낙비는 강이 되기 위해 힘쓰지 않는다.
그러나 소낙비가 쏟아지고 나면 빗물은 절로 강이 된다.
이처럼 무심히 자기 존재를 쏟아부으면
절로 존재의 꽃을 피우리라.

Flowers of existence

A sudden rain does not strive to become a river.
Yet once it falls, the waters flow into streams.
So too, if you pour forth your being with ease,
the flowers of existence will bloom in due time.

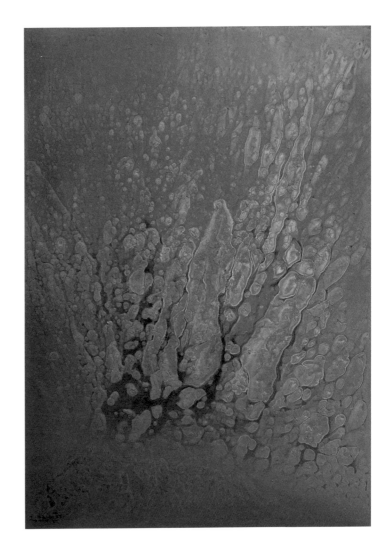

겹의풍경 – 심연 2 캔버스에 혼합물감, 72.7×100cm, 2022
'Landscapes beyond time (겹의풍경)' – Abyss 2 Mixed media on canvas, 72.7×100cm, 2022

근원의 세계

전체를 보면 옳고 그름이 없다.
부분에 머물러 자신을 괴롭히지 마라.
근원의 세계에 무슨 시비가 있으랴!

Realm of the source

In the view of the whole, right and wrong dissolve,
Do not linger in fragments, causing yourself pain.
What disputes can arise in the realm of the source?

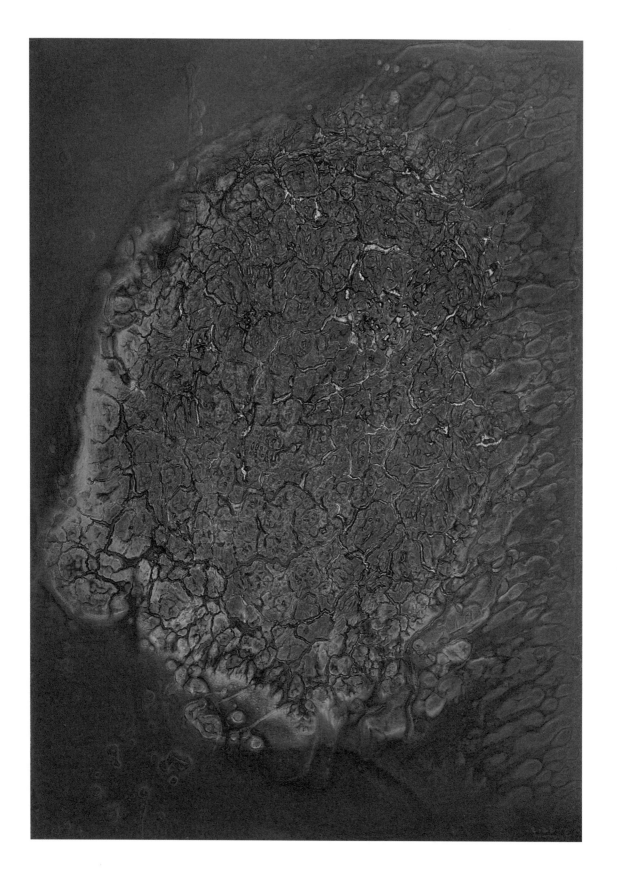

혼자 노는 사람

아무런 대상 없이 혼자 노는 사람은
밤과 낮의 구분이 없고 생과 사에도 두려움이 없다.
아무런 경계 없이 혼자 노는 사람은
어디서든 스스로 충만하다.

Playing in solitude

Those who play in solitude, without a goal,
feel neither the night's shadow nor the day's light,
unfazed by the dance of life and death.
In boundless solitude, they find their fullness,
radiant wherever they roam.

검의풍경 – 석가의 산책길(도솔천로) 캔버스에 혼합물감, 80.3x116cm, 2022
'Landscapes beyond time (검의풍경)' – The path of Buddha (Dhosol river) Mixed media on canvas, 80.3x116cm, 2022

온전한 삶

자신을 바로 보지 않고서 무엇을 의지해 살려 하는가?
자신을 정직하게 보지 않으려는 사람은
천만 성인이 길을 터줘도 온전한 삶을 살지 못한다.
어제의 말이 오늘 살아 있지 못하고
오늘의 말이 내일 살아 있지 못하면
한평생 말을 해도 아무 쓸모가 없다.

To live a complete life

What can we rely on,
if one cannot see themselves clearly?
Those who refuse to gaze upon their own truth,
even with a million sages lighting the way,
will never live a complete life.
If yesterday's words fail to breathe today,
and today's words do not echo tomorrow,
then a lifetime of speech holds no worth.

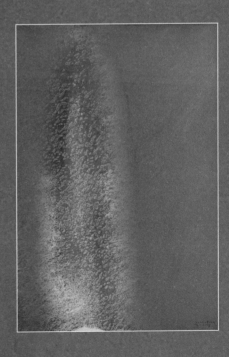

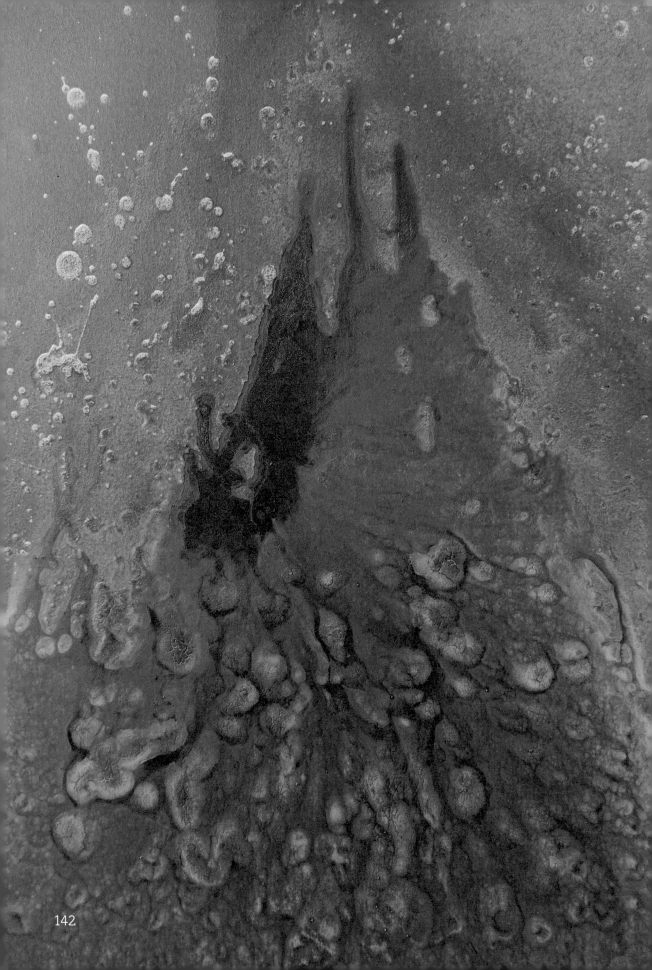

142

겹외풍경 – 태고의 신비 2 캔버스에 혼합물감, 80.3×100cm, 2022
'Landscapes beyond time (겹외풍경)' – Mysteries of primordial times 2 Mixed media on canvas, 80.3×100cm, 2022

여행의 즐거움

혼자 하는 여행은 적당히 외롭고 고독하기 마련이지만, 그러나 이 외로움과 고독은 모든
사물을 좀 더 깊이 보게 하고 좀 더 깊게 느끼게 해 준다. 그리고 나는 혼자이고 상대는 우주
공간이기 때문에 이 세상 모든 것과 일대일로 맞서지 않으면 안 된다. 고독한 일이다. 그러나
이 고독이야말로 보다 근원적인 것에 더 많은 관심을 갖게 한다. 여행의 즐거움은 새로운
풍경을 만나는 것보다 새로운 자신을 만나는 데에 있다. 더 큰 세상을 보는 것보다 더 큰
자아를 보는 것이다.

The joy of travel

Traveling alone brings a certain solitude, a loneliness that deepens the gaze and
feeling. In this quietness, I stand against the universe, facing all that exists in a
profound one-on-one. It is a solitary task, yet this solitude awakens a deeper interest
in what lies at the core. The joy of travel lies not in new landscapes, but in discovering
a new self, seeing not just a larger world, but a greater self reflected within.

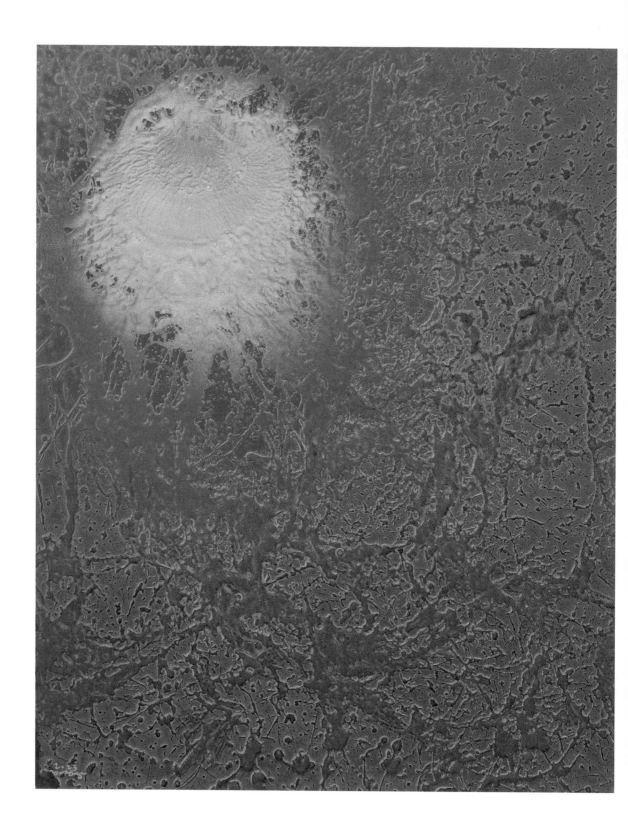

참자아의 눈뜸

고독만큼 자신을 바로 보게 하는 눈은 없다.
고독이야말로 참자아를 눈뜨게 하는 가장 큰 스승이다.
어찌 고독하지 않고서 삶과 인생을 깊이 바라볼 수 있으랴!
고독해라. 고독이야말로 세상을 온전히 품을 수 있는
강력한 힘, 사랑의 힘이다.

The awakening of the true self

None can reveal the self like solitude.
For it is loneliness that awakens the true self,
the greatest teacher in the journey of sight.
How can one gaze deeply upon life
without embracing solitude?
Cherish this solitude,
for it holds the mighty power to cradle the world;
The strength of love itself.

무심

오늘이 가기를 바라지도 않고
내일이 오기를 바라지도 않는다.
존재가 존재를 놓고 놀면
세월이 가고 오는 일이 없다.

Unconcerned

I neither wish for today to pass,
nor do I long for tomorrow's arrival.
When existence plays with existence,
time ceases to come and go.

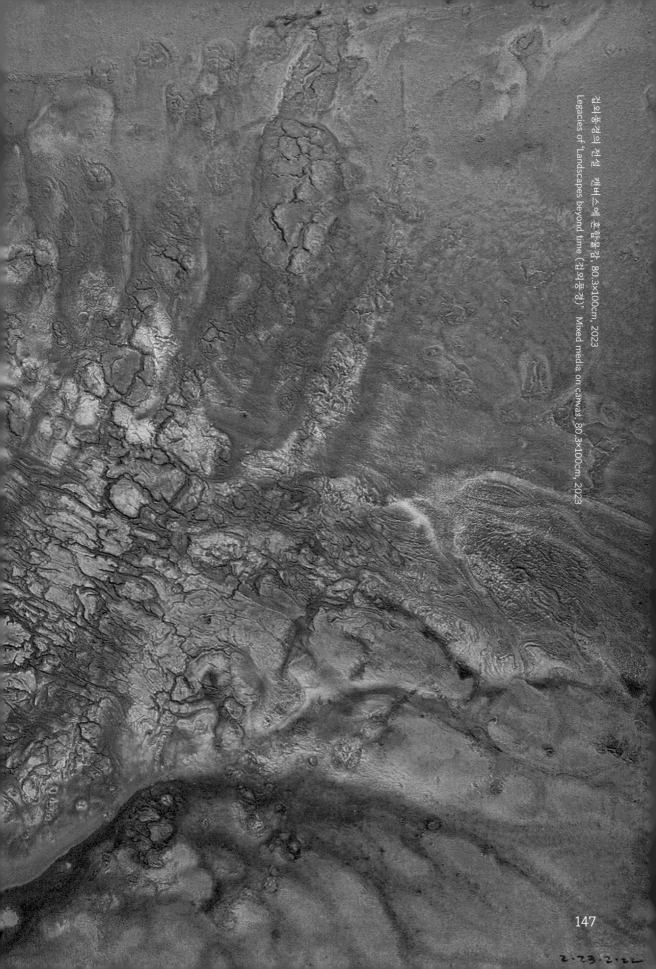

겁외풍경의 전설 캔버스에 혼합물감, 80.3×100cm, 2023
Legacies of 'Landscapes beyond time (겁외풍경)' Mixed media on canvas, 80.3×100cm, 2023

접외풍경 - 우주의 맥박 캔버스에 혼합물감, 65.2×91cm, 2022
'Landscapes beyond time (접외풍경)' - Pulse of the Cosmos   Mixed media on canvas, 65.2×91cm, 2022

예술가의 삶

예술가는 언제 어디서나
불꽃처럼 타오르는 정열이 있어야 한다.
그러나 고요히 타오르는 불꽃이어야 한다.
아무 데나 함부로 번지는 불꽃은
깊이 타지 않는다.

The life of an artist

An artist must possess a passion
that burns like a flame, fierce and bright,
Yet it should blaze with a tranquil light.
For a fire that flares without care,
will never burn with depth or grace.

정말 좋은 것은

좋은 것은 남들이 좋다고 하기 전에 좋은 줄 알아야지
남들이 좋다고 하니 우르르 따라 좋아하는 것은
좋은 것을 봐도 무엇이 좋은지 모른다.

The good things

To recognize the good before others find it so,
is to truly understand its worth.
Following the crowd in admiration,
one remains blind to its true beauty.

적멸의 아름다움

저물어가는 모든 것들은 왜 이리 아름다운지
오! 적멸의 아름다움이여,
언제 어디서나 그리운 사람 하나 있으면
한 세상 살 만하다.

The beauty of the sublime

Why do all things fading hold such beauty?
Oh! The beauty of the sublime!
If there's but one cherished soul to long for,
the world is worth living.

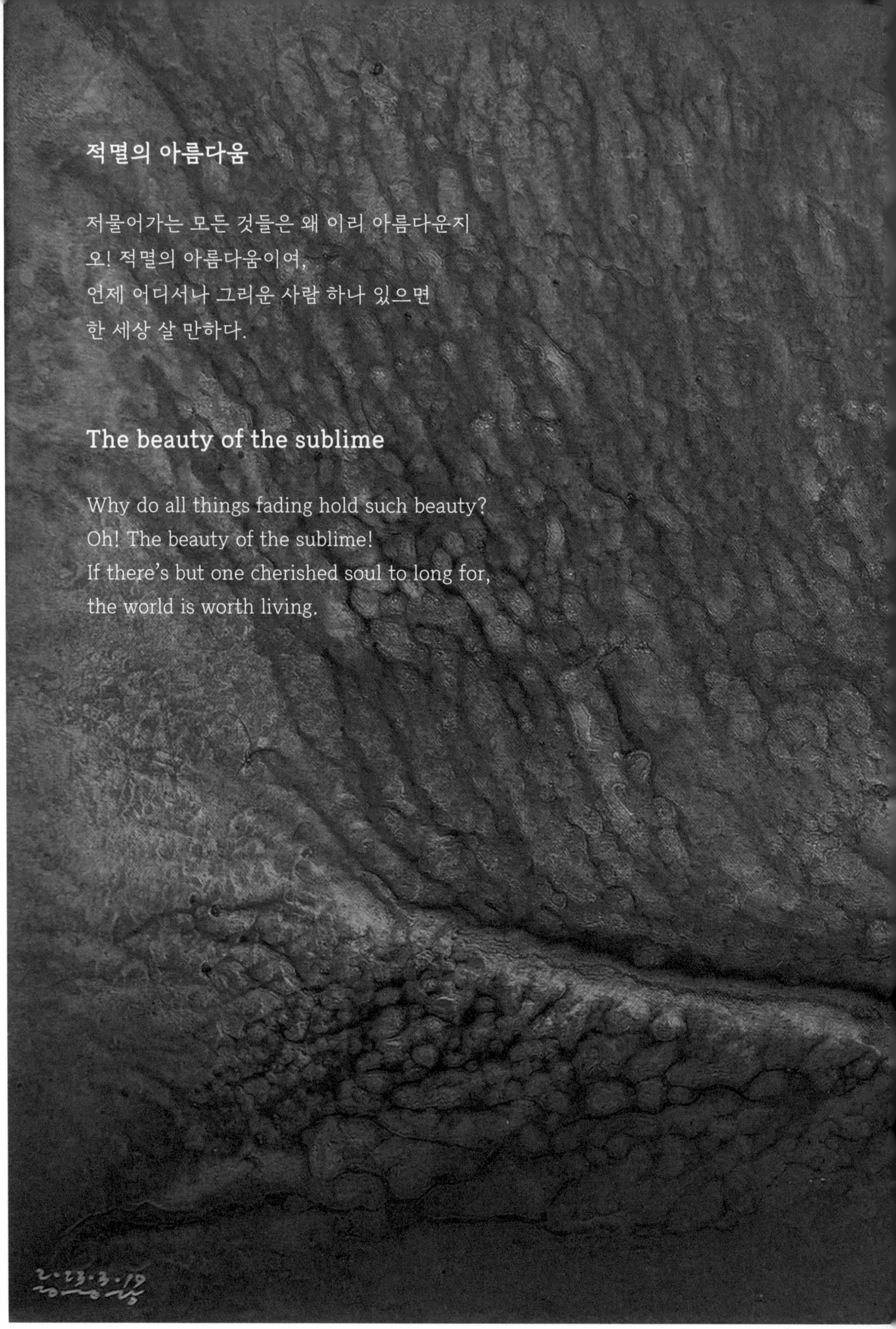

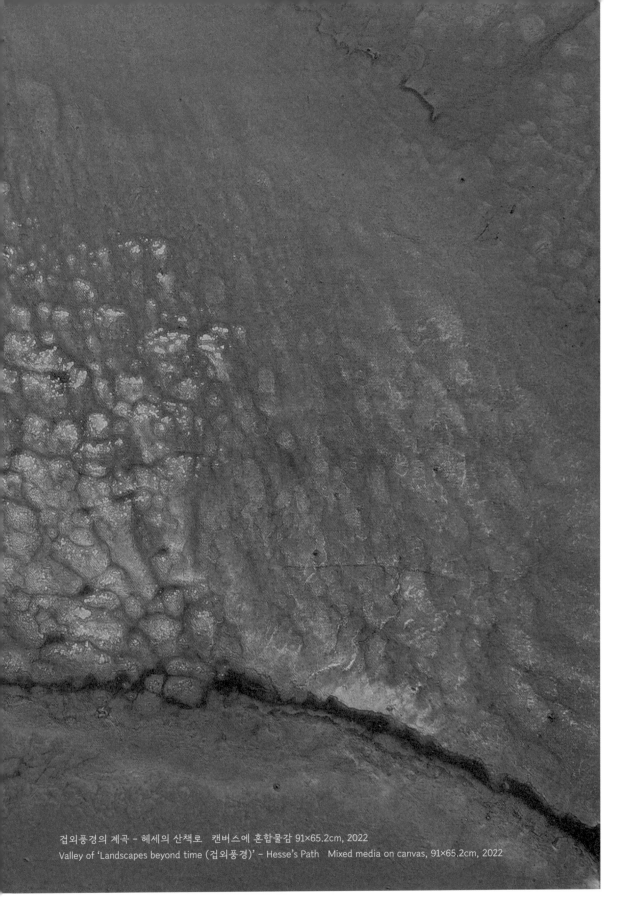

겁외풍경의 계곡 – 헤세의 산책로 캔버스에 혼합물감 91×65.2cm, 2022
Valley of 'Landscapes beyond time (겁외풍경)' – Hesse's Path   Mixed media on canvas, 91×65.2cm, 2022

밤 기차

밤 기차는 사람을 실어 나르는 것이 아니라
외로운 영혼을 실어 나른다.
밤 기차는 존재의 내면 가장 깊은 곳에서
기적을 울린다.

Night trains

The night train does not carry mere passengers,
but lonely souls upon its journey.
It rings with miracles,
from the depths of our existence's innermost core.

스스로 깨닫지 못하면

깊은 깨달음을 얻은 사람은
세상 그 어떤 언어에도 구속받지 않는다.
아무리 좋은 말도 스스로 깨닫지 못하면
자신을 구속할 뿐이다.

If they are not truly realized

A person who has found deep enlightenment
is free from the bonds of any language.
No matter how beautiful the words,
if they are not truly realized,
they only serve to bind the self.

겁외풍경 – 태고의 신비 화엄장 캔버스에 혼합물감, 72×100cm, 2022
'Landscapes beyond time (겁외풍경)' – Mysteries of primordial times, Avatamsaka Sutra
Mixed media on canvas, 72×100cm, 2022

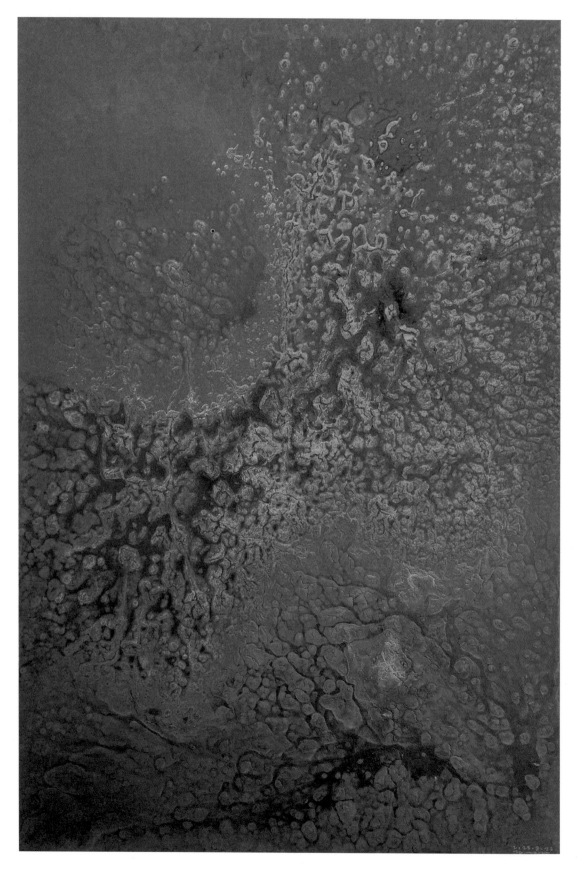

154

겨울 달

오늘 밤은 초승달이다.
날씨가 추운 탓에 소나무 가지에 걸린 초승달이
마치 손톱을 깎아 던져놓은 것처럼 날카롭게 가지를 물고 있다.
별빛이 차다. 얼어붙은 하늘이 쨍쨍 갈라진다.
달은 겨울 달이 최고, 알몸으로 산 능선을 구르는 달,
빈 나뭇가지에 걸린 달, 찬바람에 씻긴 듯 핼쑥한 달,
그리고 손을 들면 꽉 무는 달.

The winter's moon

Tonight, the crescent moon hangs low,
its sharpness clinging to the pine branches,
Like a nail clipped and cast aside.
starlight pours forth ; the frozen sky splits wide.
The moon, a winter gem, rolls over bare ridges,
a waning light caught on empty twigs,
Washed by the cold wind, it glows pale and thin,
and when I reach out, it bites back tight.

겁외풍경의 달 캔버스에 혼합물감, 80.3×116.8cm, 2022
Moon of 'Landscapes beyond time (겁외풍경)' Mixed media on canvas, 80.3×116.8cm, 2022

겹외풍경의 산 캔버스에 혼합물감, 65.2×91cm, 2022
Mountains of 'Landscapes beyond time (겹외풍경)' Mixed media on canvas, 65.2×91cm, 2022

참으로 소중한 것

숨을 쉴 때 숨 쉬어야지 하고 숨 쉬는 사람은 없다.
우리의 일상 속에는 이처럼 소중한 것들이 참 많은데
그것의 고마움을 모르고 산다.
참으로 귀하고 소중한 것은 숨이 절로 쉬어지듯
아무 말 없이 그대 곁에 머문다.
고요히 그대 곁에 머문다.

Truly precious gifts

No one breathes, thinking, 'I must take a breath.'
In our daily lives, countless treasures surround us,
Yet we wander unaware of their worth.
What is truly precious lingers quietly,
Like breath that flows without thought.
Silently, it stays beside you,
Calmly, it remains at your side.

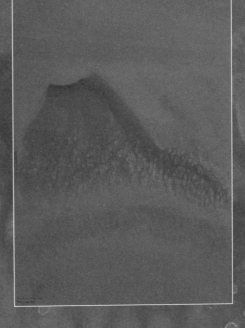

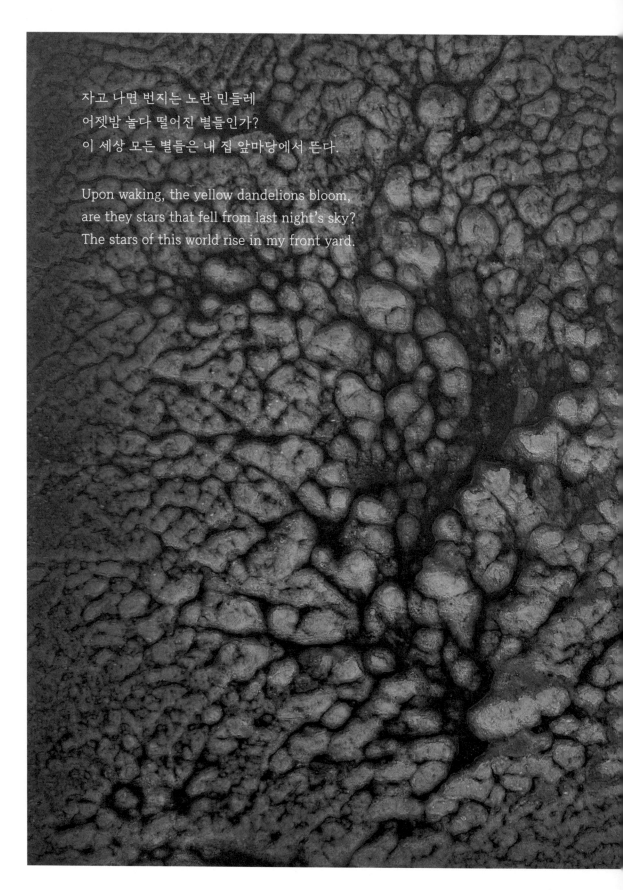

자고 나면 번지는 노란 민들레
어젯밤 놀다 떨어진 별들인가?
이 세상 모든 별들은 내 집 앞마당에서 뜬다.

Upon waking, the yellow dandelions bloom,
are they stars that fell from last night's sky?
The stars of this world rise in my front yard.

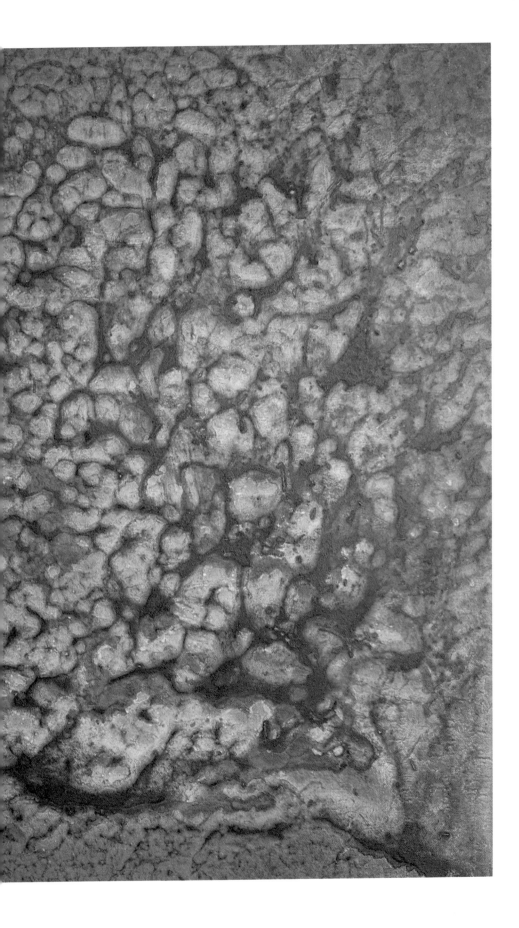

견외풍경 – 화성도, 캔버스에 혼합물감, 100×72cm, 2022
'Landscapes beyond time (견외풍경)' – Martian dust, Mixed media on canvas, 100×72cm, 2022

우리네 삶

삶이란 때론
바늘로 콕콕 찔러도 아프지 않을 때가 있고
바람 한 점 스쳐도 아플 때가 있다.

아프다는 건 살아 있다는 것.
참으로 살아 있는 사람은 바람 한 점에도
아픔이 있다는 것을 안다.

Our lives

Life, at times, is like a needle's prick,
a touch that scarcely stings,
Yet sometimes, a whisper of wind
can bring a sudden ache.

To feel pain is to be alive;
Those who truly live know well
that even the gentlest breeze,
can carry its own kind of hurt.

겹외풍경 – 신의 눈물　캔버스에 혼합물감, 91×116.8cm, 2022
'Landscapes beyond time (겹외풍경)' – Tears of the Divine
Mixed media on canvas, 91×116.8cm, 2022

가지 끝에 매달린 하늘

편백나무 숲에서 가을을 보낸다.
바람 불고 새 울 때마다 쭉쭉 찢어진다.
가지 끝에 매달린 하늘.

The sky hanging from the branches

In the cedar forest, I embrace autumn,
As the wind stirs and the birds call,
The sky, torn and stretched, hangs from the
branches.

겹외풍경 – 목성에 심은 나무   캔버스에 혼합물감, 91×116.8cm, 2022
'Landscapes beyond time (겹외풍경)' – A tree planted on Jupiter
Mixed media on canvas, 91×116.8cm, 2022

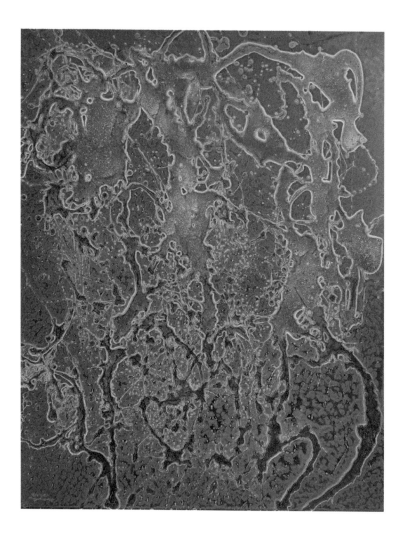

겁외풍경 – Jazz 캔버스에 혼합물감, 80.3×100cm, 2022
‘Landscapes beyond time (겁외풍경)’ – Jazz Mixed media on canvas, 80.3×100cm, 2022

무아

자신이 아무것도 아니란 걸 알면 괴로울 일도 고통스러울 일도 없다.
자신이 아무것도 아닌 줄 알면 세상과 맞서 두려울 게 없다.
자신이 아무것도 아닌 줄 알아야 걸림 없는 대자유를 누릴 수 있다.

Insignificance

When one knows they are nothing, there is no sorrow, no pain to bear.
To realize your own insignificance is to stand fearless against the world.
Only by embracing this truth can one savor the boundless freedom.

고목

큰 나무일수록 뿌리가 깊듯 아름다울수록 상처가 깊다.
상처 없는 고목이 어디 있으랴.
그러나 새가 날고 바람이 쉬어 가는 것은
상처조차 아름답기 때문이다.

The timeless tree

The taller the tree, the deeper its roots;
The more beautiful, the deeper the scars.
Where can one find a timeless tree without wounds?
Yet the birds still fly, the winds pause,
for even scars possess their own beauty.

165

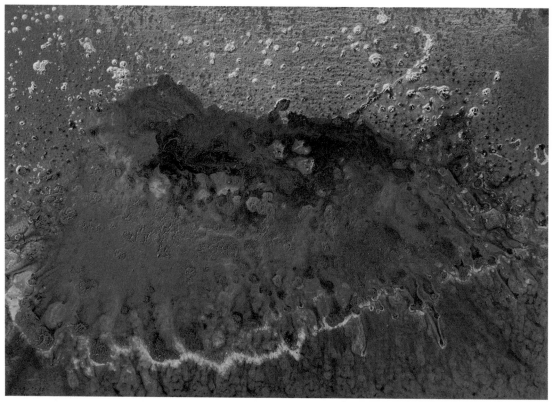

경외풍경 - 전설을 품은 바위 캔버스에 혼합물감, 100×72.7cm, 2002
'Landscapes beyond time (경외풍경)' - A rock that cradles legends
Mixed media on canvas, 100×72.7cm, 2002

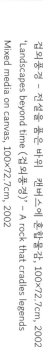

자연의 말

내 방엔 책이 없다.
그러나 내가 읽어야 할 것은 너무도 많다.
하늘에 촘촘히 박힌 말들과
산과 들에 흩어져 있는 수많은 이야기들.
자연이 내뿜는 언어는 빛과 색을 가지고
문신처럼 내 몸에 박힌다.

Nature's language

There are no books in my room,
yet there are countless words I must read.
Words scattered across the sky,
stories woven through mountains and fields.
The language of nature bursts forth,
with light and color, etching itself upon my skin like a tattoo.

겁외풍경 – 천화지언(하늘 말 땅의 언어) 캔버스에 혼합물감, 130.3×162.2cm, 2024
'Landscapes beyond time (겁외풍경)' – 천화지언 (Words of the sky, Language of the Earth) Mixed media on canvas,
130.3×162.2cm, 2024

부활

부활은 죽어 다시 태어나는 것이 아니라
산 채로 매 순간 부활하는 것이다.

Resurrection

Resurrection is not the act of dying and being reborn,
but a constant revival in each living moment.

개미가 되고 싶다

개미들은 이 더운 날씨에도 땀 한 방울 흘리지 않고
각자 하나의 우주를 물고 천하태평 잘도 논다.
개미가 되고 싶다.

I long to be an ant

Even in this sweltering heat, the ants toil without a drop of sweat,
Each cradling a universe of their own, in blissful harmony, they frolic.
I long to be an ant.

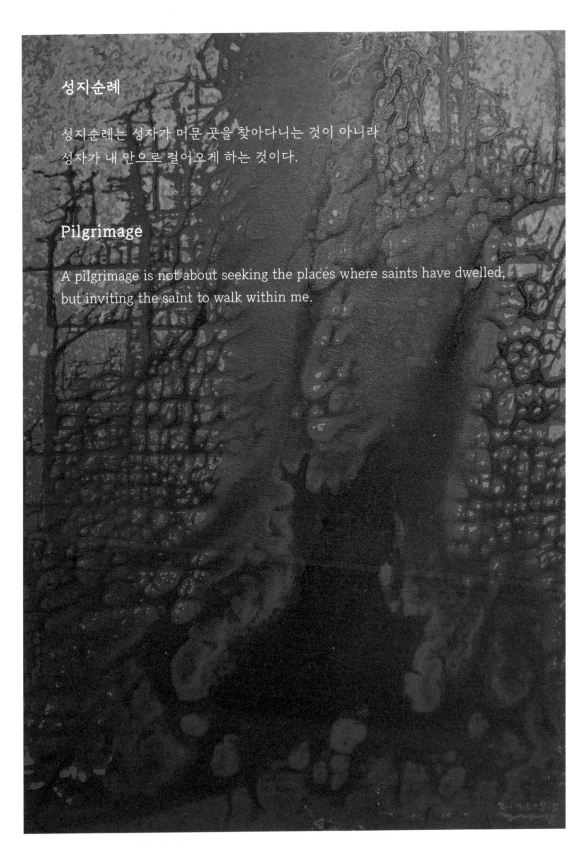

성지순례

성지순례는 성자가 머문 곳을 찾아다니는 것이 아니라
성자가 내 안으로 걸어오게 하는 것이다.

Pilgrimage

A pilgrimage is not about seeking the places where saints have dwelled,
but inviting the saint to walk within me.

겁외풍경 – 고목　캔버스에 혼합물감, 65.1×91cm, 2022
'Landscapes beyond time (겁외풍경)' – Ancient tree　Mixed media on canvas, 65.1×91cm, 2022

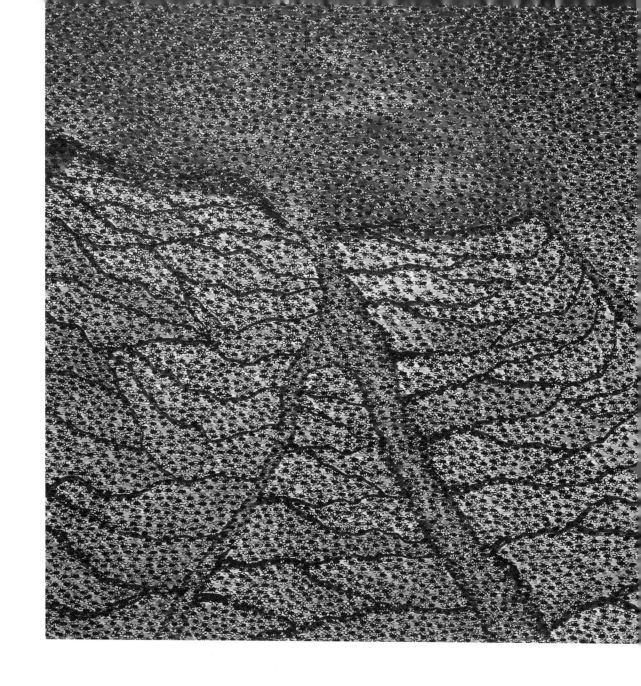

인류가 앞으로 살아갈 세상

환경 중에 가장 잘 가꾸어야 하는 것은 사람의 환경이다.
사람이 갖는 생각과 마음, 이 환경을 잘 가꾸지 않고선
다른 어떤 환경운동도 별 소용이 없다.
인류가 지금껏 살아온 세상이 신 중심, 인간 중심의 세계였다면
앞으로 살아갈 세상은 생명 중심, 환경 중심의 세계로 나아가야 한다.

바람의 기억 – 태고의 숨 화선지에 동양화물감, 185×92cm, 2015, 아프리카 여행중
Memories of the wind – Primordial breaths Oriental painting pigments on rice paper, 185×92cm, 2015, During a trip in Africa

Humanity's future

The most vital environment to nurture is that of the human heart and mind.

Without tending to this inner world, no outer movement can hold true significance.

If humanity has thrived in a world centered on the divine and the self,

we must now embrace a future grounded in the essence of life and the sanctity of

nature.

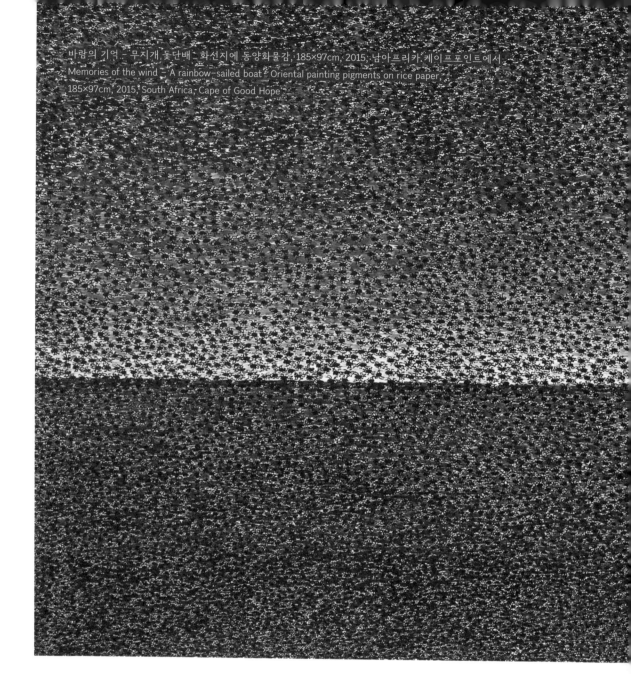

희망봉

아프리카 최남단 케이프포인트
인도양과 대서양이 만나는 곳, 희망봉에서
저 푸른 물결들을 바라보며 얼마나 많은 생각들이 스쳐갔는지
오늘 그 바다의 물결을 토해내며
그때의 감동을 다시 한번 느낀다.

172

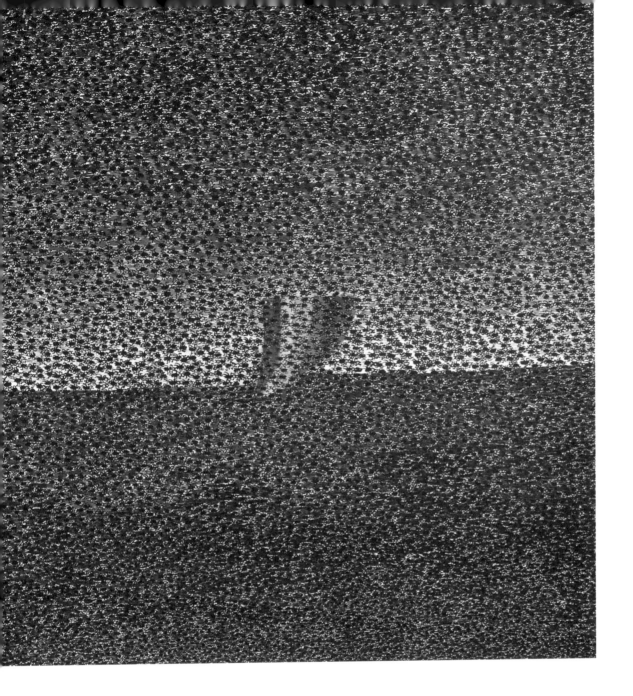

Cape of Good Hope

Standing at Cape Point, the southern tip of Africa,
where the Indian and Atlantic Oceans meet at the Cape of Good Hope,
I gaze upon the blue waves, lost in countless thoughts that have drifted by.
Today, as the sea heaves with its tides,
I once more feel the echo of that past wonder.

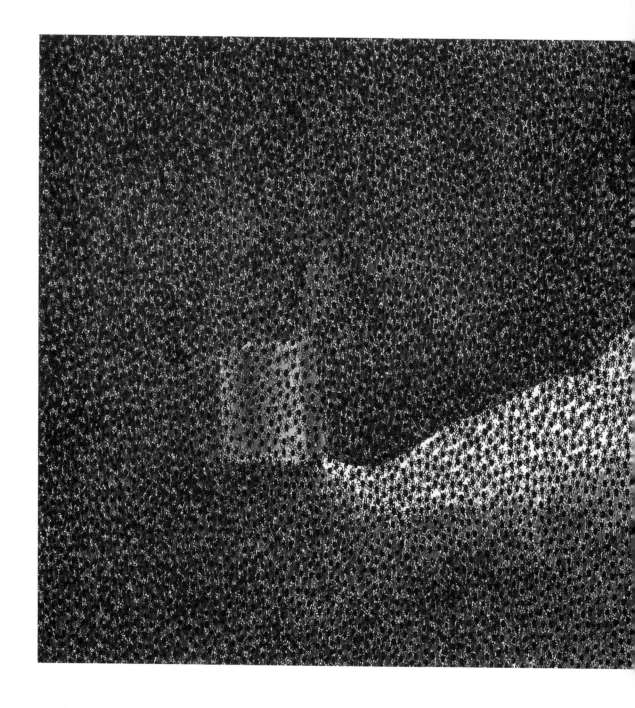

윤회

한번 친 파도가 흔적 없이 사라지는 것은
또 다른 파도로 일어나기 위함이다.
소멸하는 것을 두려워하지 마라.
또 다른 생명을 잉태하기 위함이니.

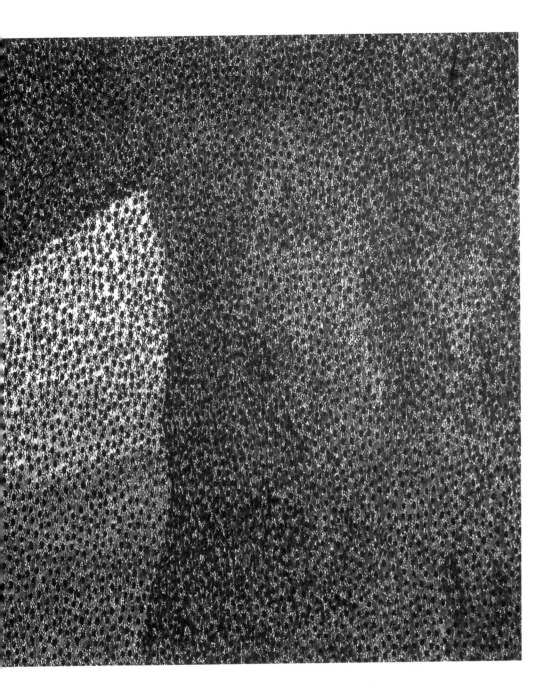

바람의 기억 – 희망· 화석지에 동양화물감, 185×97cm, 2015, 남아프리카 케이프로인드 희망봉에서
Memories of the wind – Hope Oriental painting pigments on rice paper, 185×97cm, 2015, South Africa, Cape of Good Hope

Rebirth

The wave that crashes and vanishes without a trace
is merely rising anew as another wave.
Do not fear the act of fading;
it is to give birth to yet another life.

바람의 기억 – 무지갯빛·호랑나비 화선지에 동양화물감, 185×97cm, 2015
Memories of the wind – A rainbow–hued tiger butterfly Oriental painting pigments on rice paper, 185×97cm, 2015

비움의 꽃

계절마다 돋아나는 생명의 꽃.
산은 봄엔 희망의 꽃을 피우고, 여름엔 만족의 꽃, 가을엔 결실의 꽃을 피운다.
그중에 단연 아름다운 것은 겨울, 비움의 꽃이다.
해 질 녘 으스름한 산골 풍경은 사람을 한없이 선하게 한다.
숲으로 날아드는 새들도 붉게 타오르는 노을도
산 아래 나물 캐는 아낙들의 웃음소리가 노을빛에 물든다.

The bloom of emptiness

With each season blooms the flower of life;
In spring, the mountains bear the blossom of hope,
In summer, the flower of contentment,
And in autumn, the fruit-bearing bloom.
Yet the most beautiful of all is winter's flower, the bloom of emptiness.
As dusk settles over the shadowy mountain scene,
it fills the heart with endless kindness.
Birds soar into the forest, and the crimson sunset bathes,
the laughter of women gathering herbs below in its glow.

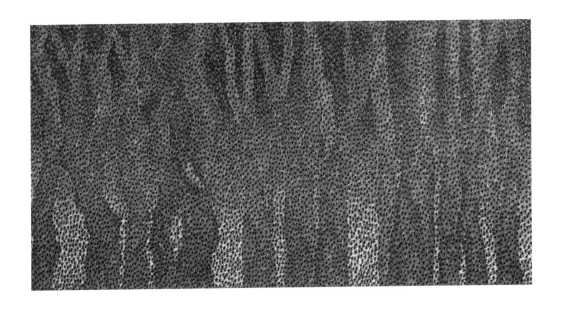

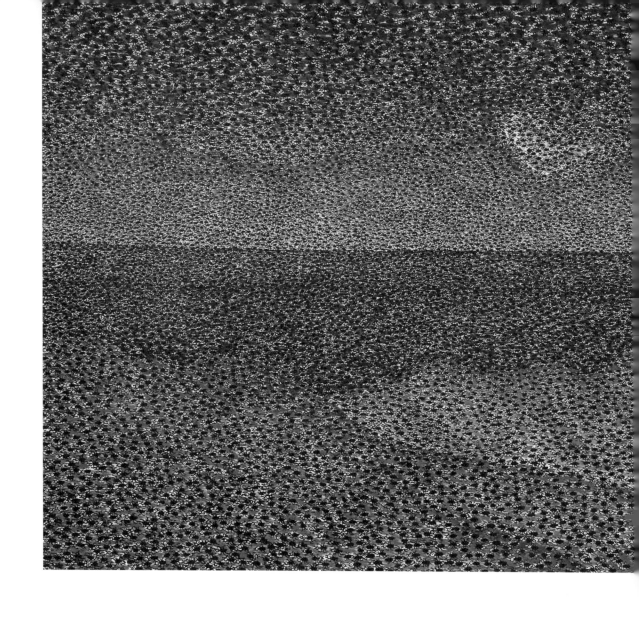

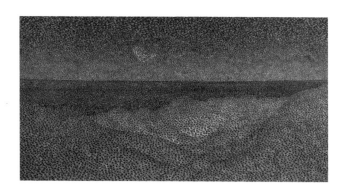

바람의 기억 – 사막의 섬
화선지에 동양화물감, 185×97cm, 2015,
아프리카 여행 중 나미비아에서
Memories of the wind – Island of the Desert
Oriental painting pigments on rice paper,
185×97cm, 2015, During a trip in Africa, Namibia

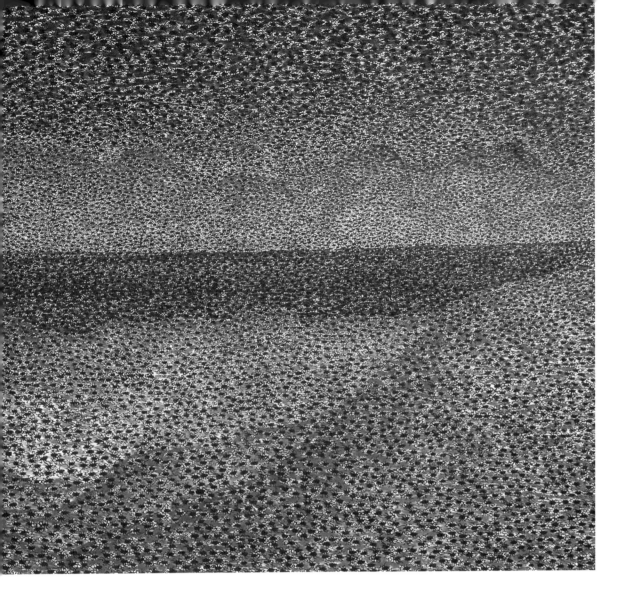

대오(大悟)

마음이란 놈이 시시각각 변하고 변하지만
크게 한번 깨친 마음은 영겁의 세월에도 변함이 없다.
방편을 좇지 말고 본질을 꿰뚫어라.

The great awakening (大悟)

The heart, ever shifting, transforms with each fleeting moment,
yet a heart that has truly awakened remains unchanged through the ages.
Do not chase after the fleeting; instead, pierce through to the essence.

선인장과 수행자

선인장과 수행자는 닮은 점이 있다.
사막에 외롭게 홀로 있는 선인장이 붉은 꽃을 피울 때 사막 전체가 붉듯이
수행자도 고독하게 홀로 있는 모습이 가장 아름답다.
그 싸늘한 눈빛이 선인장도 수행자도
무리를 이루면 빛을 잃는다.

The cactus and the seeker

The cactus and the seeker share a kinship.
When the solitary cactus blooms with red in the desert, it ignites in crimson;
So too, the seeker, in their solitude, is at their most beautiful.
In that cold gaze, both the cactus and the seeker
lose their radiance when gathered in a crowd.

경외풍경 - 별을 품은 선인장 캔버스에 혼합물감, 80.3×116.8cm, 2022, 남미 여행 중 칠레의 사막에서
'Landscapes beyond time (경외풍경)' - The cactus that cradles the stars, Mixed media on canvas, 80.3×116.8cm,
2022, During a trip to South America, in the deserts of Chile

181

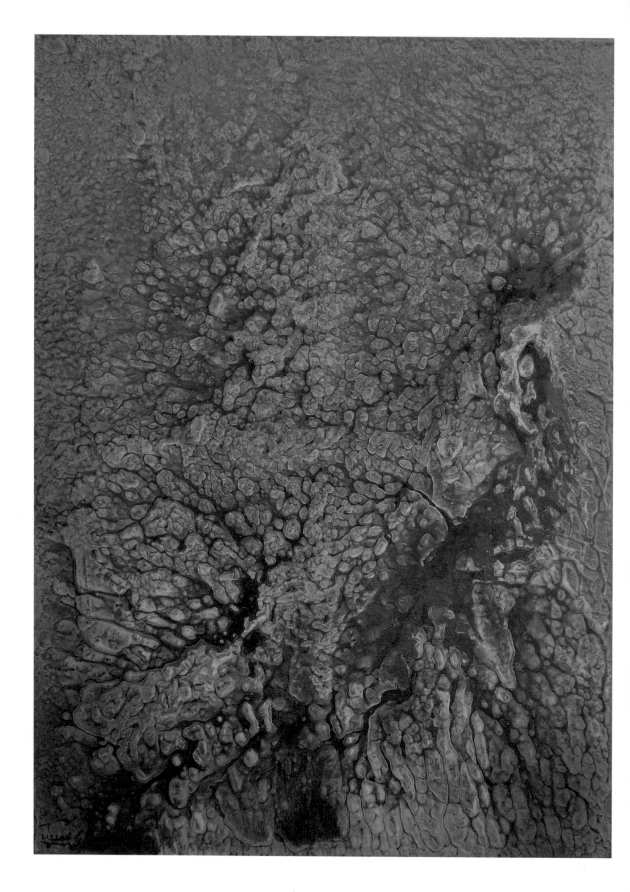

주는 기쁨

가져서 얻는 기쁨보다 주는 기쁨이 얼마나 더 행복한가.
가져서 얻는 기쁨은 가지고 난 뒤 차츰 사라지지만,
주는 기쁨은 주는 만큼 점점 더 커진다.

The joy of giving

The joy of giving surpasses the joy of receiving.
The happiness from what we possess fades away.
Yet the joy of giving blossoms, growing ever greater with each act of generosity.

겁외풍경의 가슴 캔버스에 혼합물감, 91×116.8cm, 2022
The heart of 'Landscapes beyond time (겁외풍경)' Mixed media on canvas, 91×116.8cm, 2022

견외풍경 – 빅토리아 숲 캔버스에 혼합물감, 90.3×116.8cm, 2022
'Landscapes beyond time (견외풍경)' – Victoria forest Mixed media on canvas, 90.3×116.8cm, 2022

고추잠자리

숲속에 날아든 고추잠자리
저마다 한 세계를 품고 있다.
수백 개의 세계가 충돌하지 않고
저마다 자유롭기 그지없다.

The dragonfly

The dragonflies that flit through the forest
each cradle a world of their own.
Hundreds of worlds collide without conflict,
each one living in boundless freedom.

언덕 위에 핀 꽃은 바람을 두려워하지 않는다.
사막에서 부는 바람은 쓸쓸함을 모른다.

The flower blooming on the hill fears not the wind,
for the desert wind knows not solitude.

겹외풍경 – 본지풍광(本地風光) 캔버스에 혼합물감, 65.1×91cm, 2023
'Landscapes beyond time (겹외풍경)' – The scenery of Bonji   Mixed media on canvas, 65.1×91cm, 2023

185

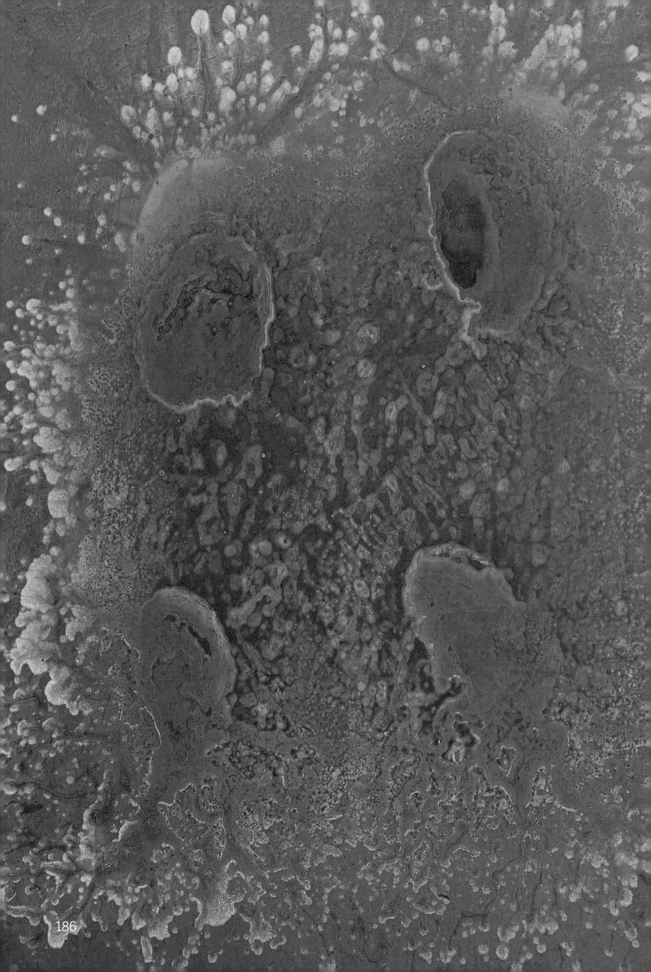

합일(合一)

내 너를 부르는 것은 단지
네 이름을 부르는 것이 아니라
세상 전부를 부르는 것이다.

내 너를 사랑하는 것은 다만
너를 사랑하는 것이 아니라
세상 전부를 사랑하는 것이다.

내 너를 부르고 사랑하는 것은
우주와 하나 되는 것이다.

Union (合一)

When I call for you, it is not just
your name that I summon,
but the entirety of the world.

When I love you, it is not merely
for you alone that my heart beats,
but for all that exists.

To call for you and to love you
is to become one with the universe.

겹외풍경 – 10.29 추모작   캔버스에 혼합물감, 91×116.8cm, 2022
'Landscapes beyond time (겹외풍경)' – 10.29 tribute
Mixed media on canvas, 91×116.8cm, 2022

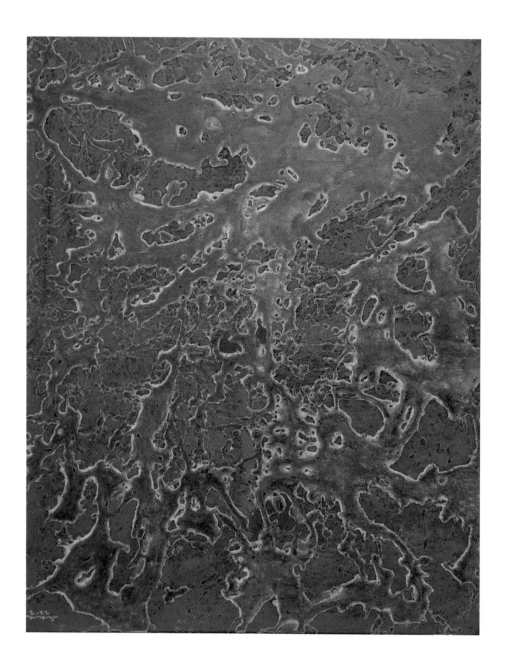

경외풍경 – Blues 캔버스에 혼합물감, 80.3×100cm, 2022
'Landscapes beyond time (경외풍경)' – Blues Mixed media on canvas, 80.3×100cm, 2022

그대의 생각도 그대의 마음도

모든 것은 흐른다.
보이는 것도 보이지 않는 것도
그대의 생각도 그대의 마음도
머물지 마라,
세상 그 어떤 것에도.

Your thoughts, your heart

All things flow,
The seen and the unseen,
Your thoughts and your heart.
Do not linger,
on anything in this world.

꿈인 줄 알아야

꿈인 줄 알고 꿈속에 사는 사람은
꿈을 꾸어도 꿈을 깨도 아무런 별일 없고
모르는 사람은 꿈에서도 꿈 밖에서도 항상 별일이 많다.
꿈만 꿈이 아니요 생시도 꿈인 줄 알아야
더 이상 꿈꾸지 않는다.

Knowing it's a dream

The one who lives within a dream,
knowing it's a dream, finds no trouble in waking.
But the unaware are burdened with endless trials,
both in dreams and in waking life.
To realize that not only dreams are dreams,
but that life itself is but a dream,
is to awaken from all dreaming.

겹외풍경 – 고흐의 꿈 캔버스에 혼합물감, 91×116.8cm, 2022
'Landscapes beyond time (겹외풍경)' – Dreams of Gogh Mixed media on canvas, 91×116.8cm, 2022

무엇이 와도 놓고 놀아라

부처가 오면 부처를 놀고 중생이 오면 중생을 놀고
사랑이 오면 사랑을 놀고 미움이 오면 미움을 논다.
삶이 오면 삶을 놀고 죽음이 오면 죽음을 논다
과연 그대는 죽음이 오면 죽음을 놀 수 있겠는가?

Whatever shall come, just dance on

When the Buddha comes, we play with the Buddha;
When sentient beings arrive, we dance with them.
With love, we embrace love;
And with hate, we engage in hate.
When life arrives, we revel in life;
And when death approaches, we discuss death.
But tell me, can one truly frolic with death when it comes?

겹외풍경 – 빈 마음의 노래   캔버스에 혼합물감, 91×116.9cm, 2023
'Landscapes beyond time (겹외풍경)' – Hymns of the empty soul   Mixed media on canvas, 91×116.9cm, 2023

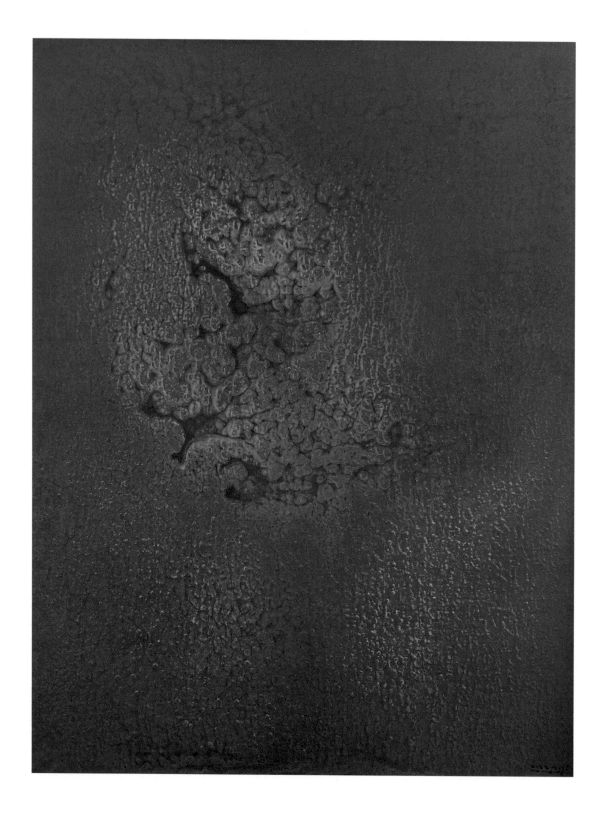

겁외풍경 – 아인슈타인의 고뇌 캔버스에 혼합물감, 91×116.8cm, 2023
'Landscapes beyond time (겁외풍경)' – The anguish of Einstein Mixed media on canvas, 91×116.8cm, 2023

고뇌하는 사람

고뇌하는 사람은 아름답다.
고뇌하는 사람은 물질세계를 넘어 영혼의 세계에 눈 맞춘다.
고통받는 삶은 집착과 욕망이 그 원인이고
고뇌하는 삶은 진리에 대한 그리움이 그 원인이다.
고뇌하는 사람이 아름다운 것은
진리에 대한 그리움에 사무쳐 있기 때문이다.

The one who suffers

The one who suffers is beautiful,
for in their anguish, they gaze beyond the material,
finding focus in the realm of the soul.
A life of pain stems from attachment and desire,
while a life of sorrow is born from a longing for truth.
The beauty of the anguished lies in their deep yearning for that very truth.

윤회의 강

윤회의 강에서 몸을 씻고
새끼손가락으로 강을 튕기니
배를 안 타고도 강을 건너네.

오호! 강 건너 저 늙은이는
무슨 일로 서 있는가?

The river of rebirth

Washing my body in the river of rebirth,
I flick the waters with my pinky,
crossing the river without a boat.

Oh! What is that old man doing,
standing over there on the other shore?

겁외풍경 – 윤회의 강 캔버스에 혼합물감, 80.3×116.8cm, 2023
'Landscapes beyond time (겁외풍경)' – River of rebirth. Mixed media on canvas, 80.3×116.8cm, 2023

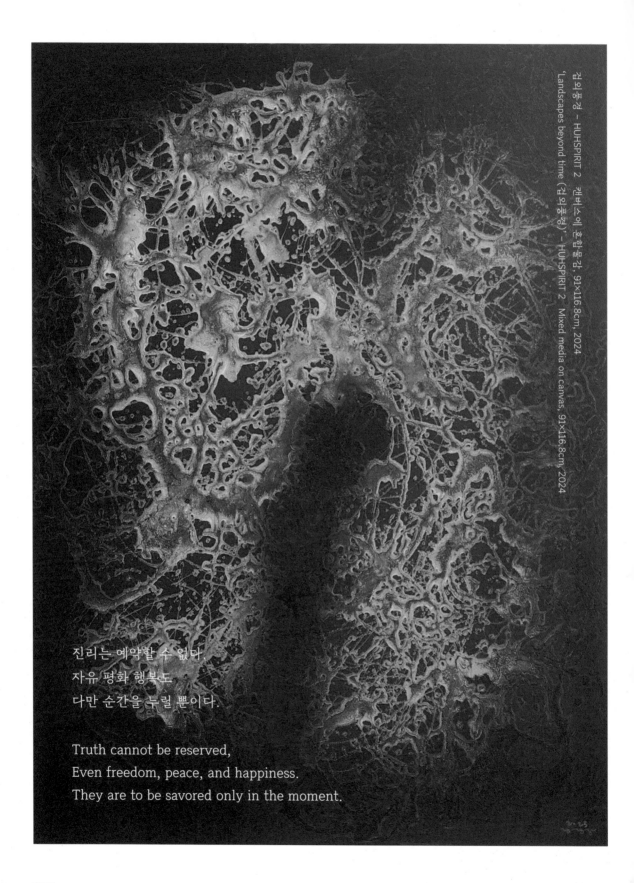

겹의풍경 – HUHSPIRIT 2 캔버스에 혼합물감, 91x116.8cm, 2024
'Landscapes beyond time (겹의풍경)' – HUHSPIRIT 2 Mixed media on canvas, 91x116.8cm, 2024

진리는 예약할 수 없다,
자유 평화 행복도
다만 순간을 누릴 뿐이다.

Truth cannot be reserved,
Even freedom, peace, and happiness.
They are to be savored only in the moment.

196

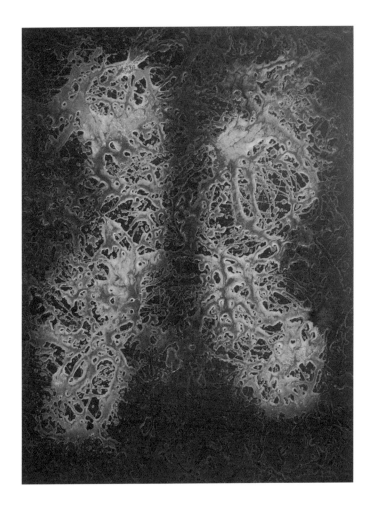

겁외풍경 - 깨어 있는 고통 캔버스에 혼합물감, 91×116.8cm, 2023
'Landscapes beyond time (겁외풍경)' - Awakened suffering Mixed media on canvas, 91×116.8cm, 2023

자기 선언

예술은 오롯한 자신의 삶의 풍경이다.
"나는 이렇게 살았노라."
자기 선언을 확실히 하는 예술가가
많아지기를 원한다.

Self-declaration

Art is the landscape of one's authentic life.
'I have lived this way,'
May the number of artists
who boldly declare themselves, continue to grow.

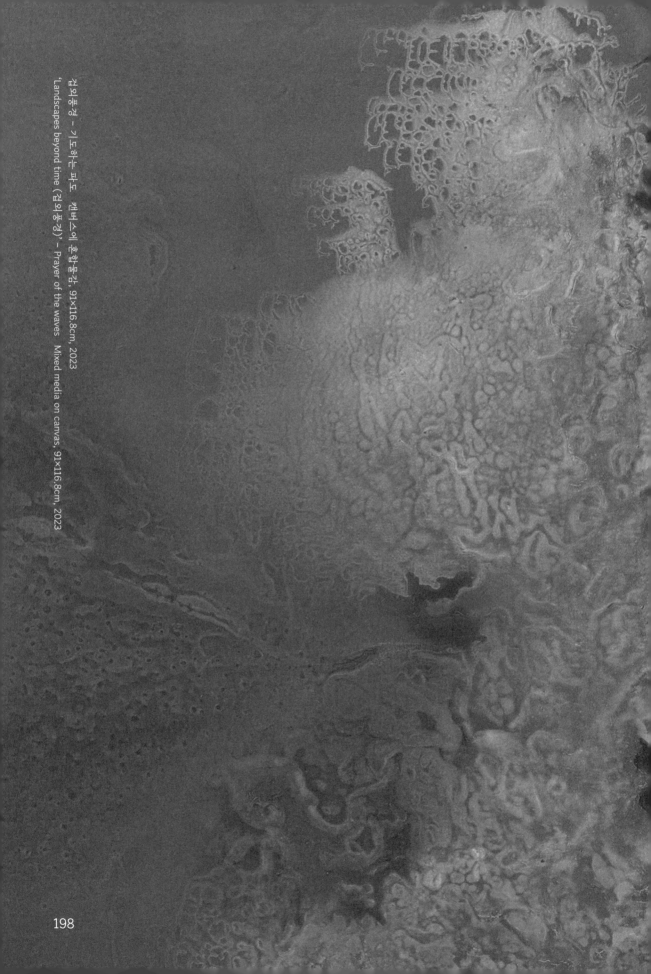

'경외풍경 – 기도하는 파도, 캔버스에 혼합물감, 91x116.8cm, 2023
'Landscapes beyond time〈경외풍경〉 - Prayer of the waves Mixed media on canvas, 91x116.8cm, 2023

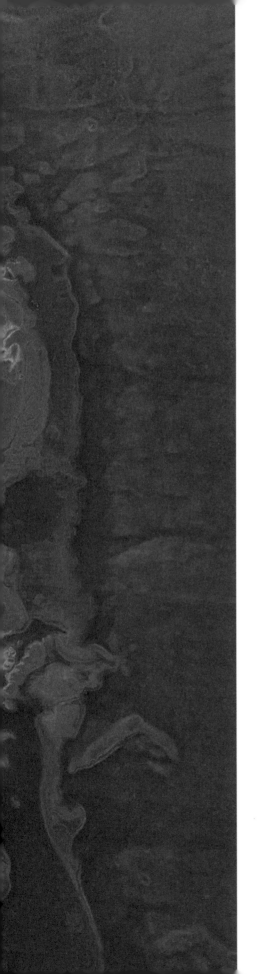

홀로 있다는 것은

홀로 있다는 것은
우주가 통째로 내게 말을 거는 순간.
깨달음이란 이 순간을 지켜보며
고요히 응답하는 것.

To be alone

To be alone is
to hear the universe speaking to me.
And enlightenment is to quietly respond,
watching over this moment.

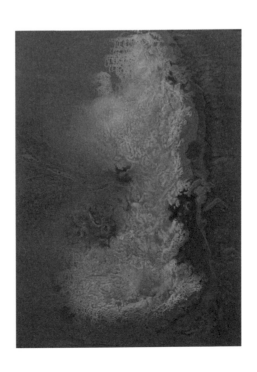

조직은 진리를 말하지 않고 집단은 진실을 말하지 않는다
자유 진리 생명 이것을 조직할 사람은 아무도 없다.

Organizations do not speak the truth, and groups do not voice reality.
No one is left to organize freedom, truth, and life.

겹외풍경 – 심연   캔버스에 혼합물감, 80.3×100cm, 2022
'Landscapes beyond time (겹외풍경)' – Abyss   Mixed media on canvas, 80.3×100cm, 2022

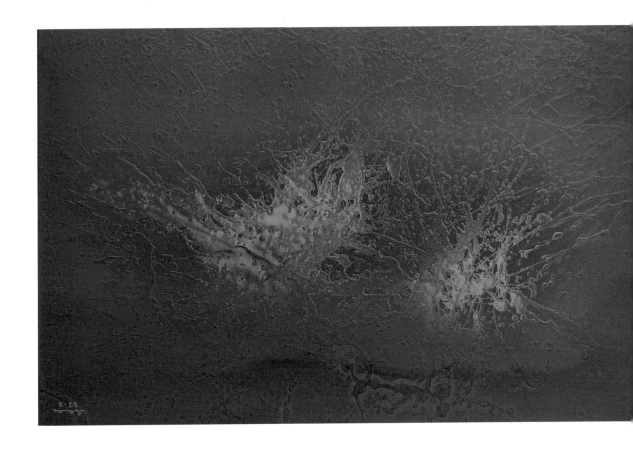

이 마음 하나면

있어도 자만하지 않고 없어도 비굴하지 않은 마음
있어도 넘치지 않고 없어도 부족함이 없는 마음
이 마음 하나면 천하를 갖고 논다.

With such a heart

A heart that remains humble in abundance and steadfast in absence,
A heart that knows no excess in plenty and feels no lack when withdrawn,
With such a heart, one can play with the world.

겁외풍경 – 환희용약 캔버스에 혼합물감, 100×80.3cm, 2023
'Landscapes beyond time (겁외풍경)' – Elixir of joy   Mixed media on canvas, 100×80.3cm, 2023

나무가 말했다

살아도 살지 못하고 죽어도 죽지 못한 것은
존재 그 자체로 온전하지 못한 까닭.
작년에 심은 나무가 아무 말 없이 죽고
올봄에 심은 나무가 아무 말 없이 산다.
나무가 말했다. 인간은 온전히 죽지도 살지도 못하면서
하루에 골백번 더 죽고 산다고.

The tree speaks

To live yet not truly live, to die yet not fully die,
this is the fault of existence itself.
As last year's tree fades quietly away,
while this spring's sapling flourishes in silence.
The tree speaks: humans, unable to fully die or live,
ressurect a hundred times each day.

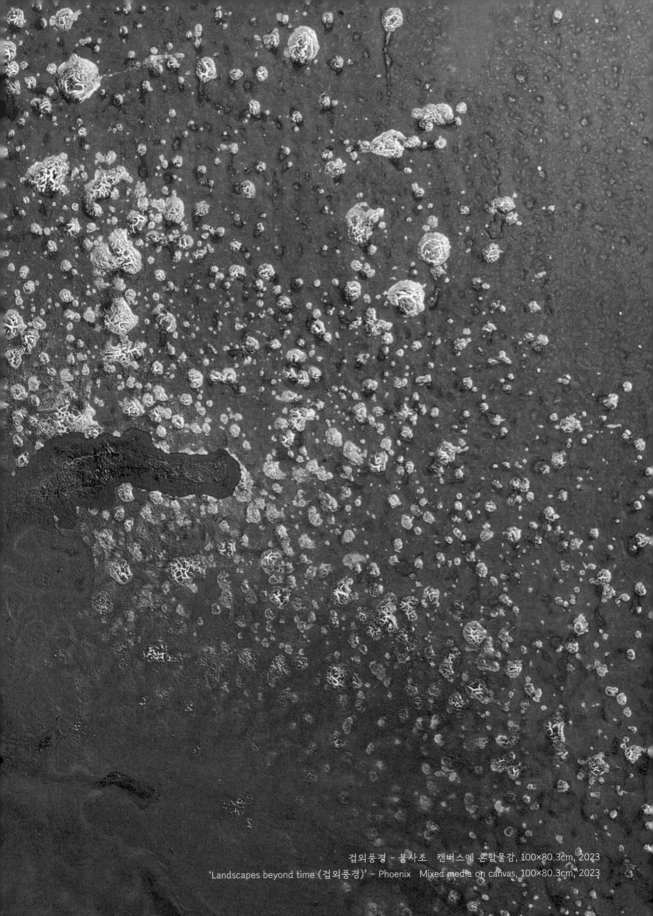

겁외풍경 – 불사조 캔버스에 혼합물감, 100×80.3cm, 2023
'Landscapes beyond time (겁외풍경)' – Phoenix Mixed media on canvas, 100×80.3cm, 2023

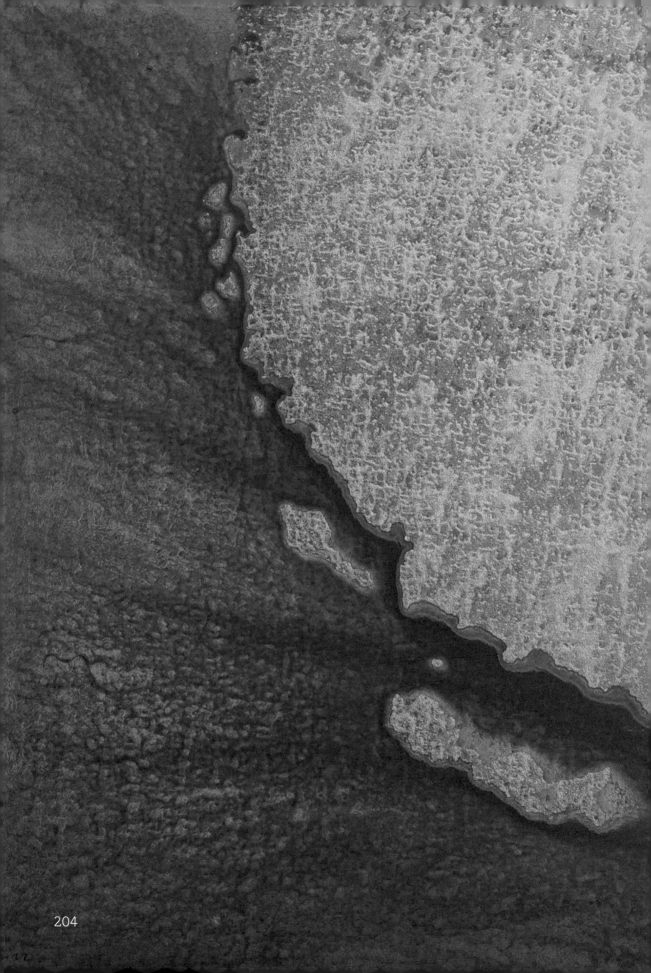

추억 여행

한국에서 보면 아르헨티나는 지구 남쪽의 끝, 노르웨이는 북쪽의 끝이다.
끝에서 끝을 보는 게 좋아 남쪽의 끝 아르헨티나 우수아이아에서
약 15일간 머물다 오늘 북쪽의 끝 노르웨이 노르카프로 왔다.
추억 여행은 현지에서 느꼈던 것보다 더 많은 것을 상상하고
더 섬세한 아름다움을 느낄 수 있어 참 좋다.
특히 그림을 그릴 때에는 그때 보지 못한 것들,
그냥 스쳐 지나간 것들까지 분명하게 손끝에 와닿는다.

A journey of reminiscence

From Korea, Argentina lies at the southern tip of the Earth,
while Norway stands at the northern edge.
I delight in seeking ends, spending about fifteen days in Argentina's Ushuaia,
before journeying today to the northern shores of Norway, to Nordkapp.
This trip through countless memories brings forth,
more than what I have felt in the moment,
revealing a delicate beauty that enriches my heart.
Especially when I paint, the unseen and the fleeting,
Which were once just whispers, now vividly touch the tips of my fingers.

겹외풍경 - 노르카프의 언덕 1 캔버스에 혼합물감, 72.7×90.9cm, 2022
'Landscapes beyond time (겹외풍경)' – The hills of Nordkapp 1 Mixed media on canvas, 72.7×90.9cm, 2022

정말 좋은 풍경은

그림을 그리는 사람이라면
여행 중 정말 좋은 풍경은 사진을 찍지 말고 가슴에 품어오는 것이 좋다.
사진을 찍어버리면 사진을 보는 순간 '아, 내가 거길 갔다 왔구나' 정도의 생각에 멈출 뿐,
그 풍경이 갖고 있는 비밀한 생명세계의 신비와 그리움이 사라져
그 속에 숨어 있는 무한한 생명의 아름다움을 놓쳐버리기에…
정말 좋은 풍경은 가슴속 그리움으로 남겨두는 것이 좋다.

The beauty of a landscape so fine

For those who paint,
It's best to carry the beauty of a landscape so fine,
in our hearts, rather than capturing it in a photograph.
For once the picture is taken,
we merely think, 'Ah, I've been there,'
losing the secret, vibrant life and the longing that the scene holds,
missing the infinite beauty concealed within.
Truly great landscapes should remain as a cherished yearning in our souls.

겹의 풍경 - 노르카프의 언덕 2 캔버스에 혼합물감, 91×65.2cm, 2022
'Landscapes beyond time〈겹의 풍경〉- The hills of Nordkapp 2 Mixed media on canvas, 91×65.2cm, 2022

크레타섬

그리스 크레타섬을 두 번 갔다 왔다. 물고기 한 마리가 편안히 누워 있는 것 같은
길쭉한 섬, 나에게 최초로 땅의 슬픔과 기쁨을 느끼게 한 곳, 땅의 슬픔은 내 삶을
자비롭게 했고 땅의 기쁨은 내 삶을 열정으로 치솟게 했다. 알 수 없는 큰 슬픔과 큰
기쁨은 세월이 지나면서 내 안의 모든 두려움을 떨쳐냈다.

삶과 죽음도 조르바의 해학처럼 그냥 하나의 웃음거리 농담일 뿐, 별 의미가
없었다. 하지만 의미 없이 아름다운 것이 가장 아름답다는 것을 깨달았다.
묘하게도 슬프고 묘하게도 기뻤던 크레타섬의 추억을 오늘 조르바를 생각하며
그렸다.

참 오래 품었다.
크레타!

Crete

I have visited the Greek island of Crete twice, a long, slender isle where a fish
seems to rest in peace. It was here that I first felt the land's sorrow and joy;
the land's sorrow brought mercy to my life, while its joy ignited my passion.
unfathomable depths of sadness and joy have, over time, shaken off all my fears.

Life and death, like Zorba's humor, turn into mere jests, devoid of meaning.
Yet I learned that the most beautiful things are those that exist without purpose.
Today, reflecting on Zorba, I painted memories of Crete – Strangely sad, yet
beautifully joyful.

How long I have cherished this place.
Ah, Crete!

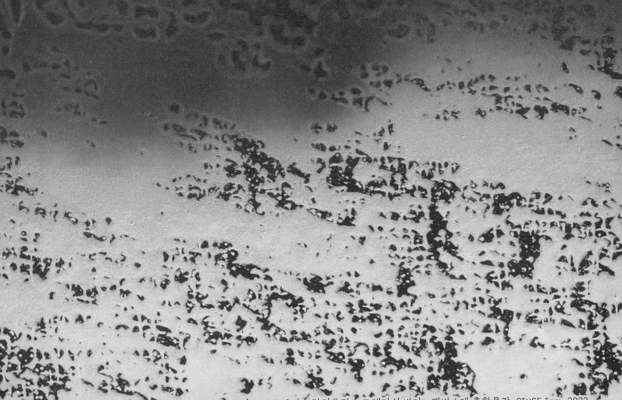

겹외풍경 – 크레타섬 바다〉 캔버스에 혼합물감, 91×65.1cm, 2022
'Landscapes beyond time (겹외풍경)' – Oceans of Crete Mixed media on canvas, 91×65.1cm, 2022

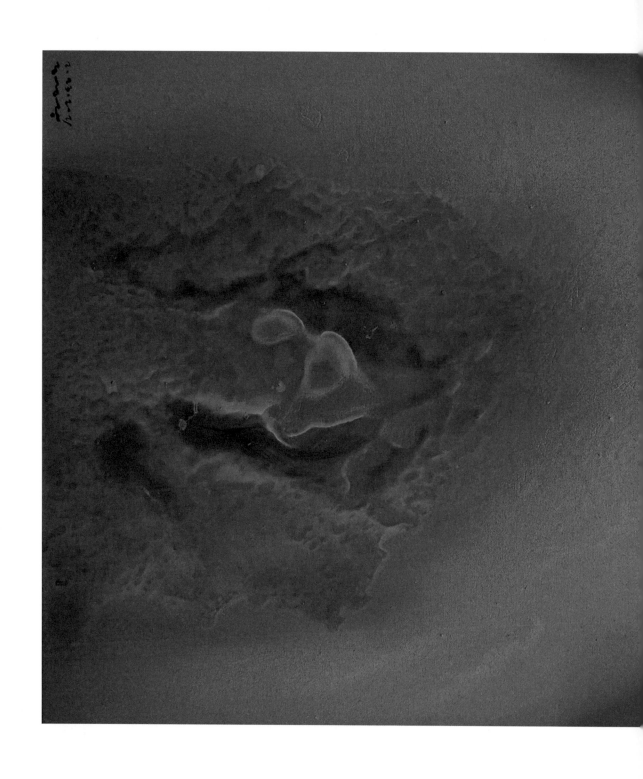

겁외풍경 – 천지창조　캔버스에 혼합물감, 65.2×91cm, 2023
'Landscapes beyond time (겁외풍경)' – The creation　Mixed media on canvas, 65.2×91cm, 2023

깨어 있어라

예술적 영감은 어디서 오는가?
깨어 있는 마음에서 온다.
깨어 있어라.
지금 깨어 있는 그대의 마음이
천지창조다.

Stay awake

From where does artistic inspiration arise?
It comes from a heart that is awake.
Stay awake.
The heart that is present in this moment,
is the very essence of creation.

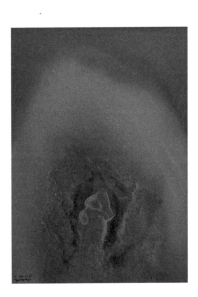

사람인 까닭에

사람이 사람인 까닭에 외롭기도 하고 고독하기도 하다.
사람이 사람인 까닭에 아프기도 하고 슬프기도 하다.
사람이 사람인 까닭에 사랑도 하고 이별도 한다.
그러나 이 모든 것에 집착하지 않고 툭 놓고 놀 줄 알면
자신의 존재가 스스로 빛난다.

Because we are human

Because we are human, we feel loneliness and solitude.
Because we are human, we endure pain and sorrow.
Because we are human, we love and part ways.
Yet if we can let go of all these attachments,
Our very existence will begin to shine.

겁외풍경 – 노래하는 바위 캔버스에 혼합물감, 80.3×100cm, 2023
'Landscapes beyond time (겁외풍경)' – Singing stones Mixed media on canvas, 80.3×100cm, 2023

무심 화선지에 동양화물감, 49×62cm, 2010
Unmindful stillnes Oriental painting pigments on rice paper, 49×62cm, 2010

세상이 혼란스러운 것은

사람을 대할 때 가르치려 하지 마라.
세상이 혼란스러운 것은 배우고자 하는 사람은 그리 많지 않은데
가르치려고 하는 사람이 너무 많기 때문이다.

A world of chaos

When meeting others, seek not to teach.
The world is chaotic, not for the lack of eager learners,
but because there are too many, who wish to teach.

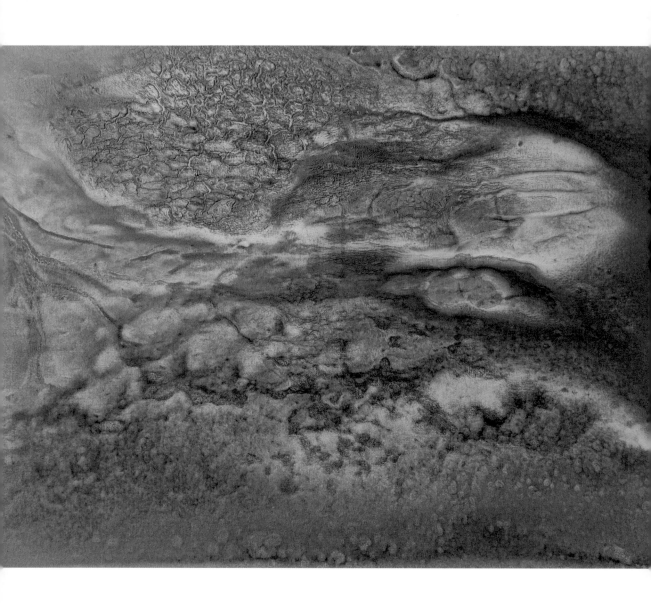

마음을 비우면

세상에 당신이 소유할 수 있는 것은 아무것도 없다.
다만 세상과 벗하며 살아갈 뿐.
마음을 비우면 삶에서 일어나는 모든 것이 신비롭다.
마음을 비우면 나는 나, 그것만이 내가 아니라
나를 바라보는 모든 것이 이미 나이다.
마음을 비우면 거짓된 나는 사라지고
하나의 큰 생명이 존재한다.
내가 없으면 모든 것이 온전하다.

An empty heart

In this world, there is nothing you can truly possess;
you simply walk alongside it,
and when your heart is empty,
all that arises in life becomes a mystery.
With an empty heart, I am not just I;
everything that gazes upon me is already a part of me.
When the false self fades away,
a great, singular life remains.
Without me, all is whole.

겁외풍경 – 화석 물고기 캔버스에 혼합물감, 100×72.7cm, 2023
'Landscapes beyond time (겁외풍경)' – Fossilized fish   Mixed media on canvas, 100×72.7cm, 2023

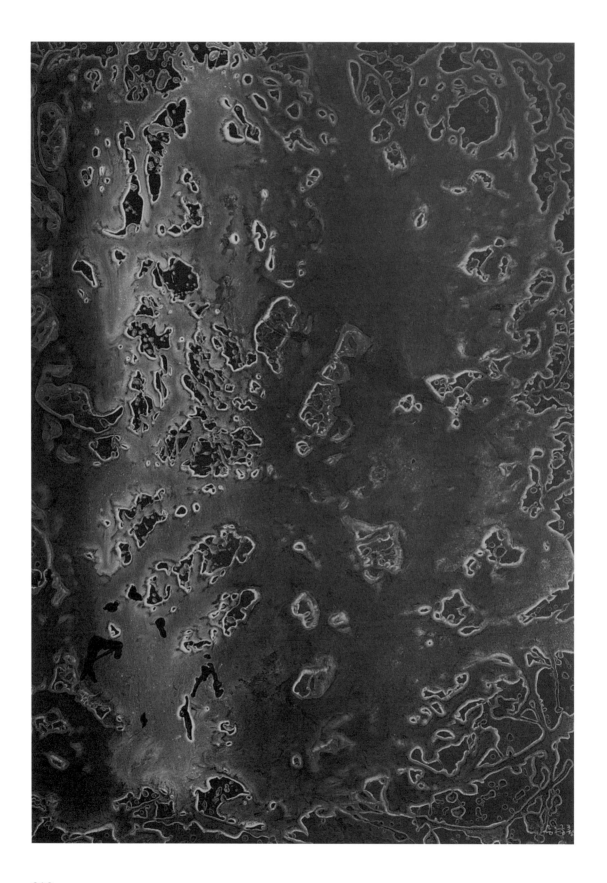

겹외풍경 – 고독의 끝 캔버스에 혼합물감, 80.3×116.8cm, 2023
'Landscapes beyond time (겹외풍경)' – The end of loneliness   Mixed media on canvas, 80.3×116.8cm, 2023

각자의 슬픔과 자비

다 알고도 다 아는 이야기를
다 하지 못하는 것이 각자(覺者)의 가장 큰 슬픔이요
이 세상이 참으로 헛되고 꿈속의 꿈이요
도깨비 장난인 줄 알면서도
그 꿈을 함께하는 것이 참으로 진정한
각자(覺者)의 자비이다.

The sorrows and compassions of the awakened

To know it all yet leave some truths unsaid;
This is the sorrow of the awakened ones (覺者).
This world is truly hollow, a dream within a dream,
a playful trick of the spirits.
Yet to share in this dream;
This is the compassion of the awakened (覺者).

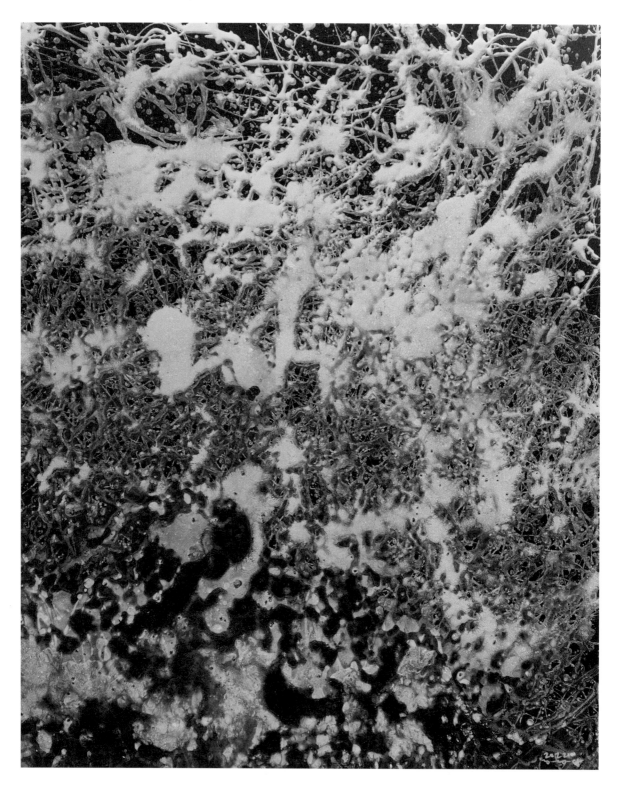

겹외풍경 – 겨울바람 1 캔버스에 혼합물감, 80.3×100cm, 2022
'Landscapes beyond time (겹외풍경)' – Winter's whispers 1 Mixed media on canvas, 80.3×100cm, 2022

내 살아 있는 동안

괜찮다, 울어도 울어도 괜찮다.
세상에 울지 않는 자 아무도 없다.
괜찮다, 슬퍼도 슬퍼도 괜찮다.
세상에 슬픔 없는 자 아무도 없다.

괜찮다, 외로워도 고독해도.

살아서 울지 않는 자 아무런 사랑 없고
살아서 슬픔 없는 자 아무런 기쁨 없다.
살아서 외로움 없는 자 아무런 삶의 의미 없고
살아서 고독하지 않은 자 인생이랄 것도 없다.

괜찮다, 조금 불행해도 행복해도.
내 살아 있는 동안.

For as long as I live

It's okay to cry, even if the tears flow endlessly.
No one in this world can escape the weeping.
It's okay to feel sorrow; sadness is part of being.
In this world, none exist without sorrow.

It's okay to be lonely, to feel the weight of solitude.

Those who live without tears know none of love,
And those who live without sorrow find no joy.
Life devoid of loneliness holds no meaning,
And those who aren't lonely have no life at all.

It's okay to feel a little unhappy, or to know happiness,
For as long as I live, it's all part of the journey.

겁외풍경 – 겨울바람 2   캔버스에 혼합물감, 72.7×100cm, 2022
'Landscapes beyond time (겁외풍경)' – Winter's whispers 2   Mixed media on canvas, 72.7×100cm, 2022

텅 빈 계곡

동네 개 짖는 소리가 이 산 저 산에서 꽁꽁 얼어붙는다.
겨울은 다른 어떤 계절보다 사람의 영혼을 맑게 해주는 묘한 힘을 가지고 있다.
텅 빈 계곡에 발을 담그면 맑은 하늘이 정수리에 꽂힌다.

The empty valley

The sounds of dogs barking in the village freeze across the mountains,
For winter holds a strange power, clearing the soul more than any other season.
When I step into the empty valley, the clear sky pierces my crown.

만행

바랑 하나 둘러메고 길 떠나던 날
무심의(無心衣) 갈아입고 좋아했었네.
옷깃에 별을 달고 달을 달아서
밤길 홀로 선 걸음도 시원해라.
한 걸음 부처 나고 두 걸음 부처 나네.
오호라! 한세월 억만 겁을 돌아서
한 걸음 두 걸음 억만 부처 만나리,

Endless journey

On the day I set out with a single pack,
I donned the robes of unmindfulness with joy.
With stars pinned to my collar and the moon at my side,
each solitary step through the night feels refreshing.
With one step, the Buddha is born; with two, the Buddha arises.
Oh! After countless eons have passed,
with each step, I shall meet a million Buddhas.

겁외춘경 – 언덕의 노래 캔버스에 혼합물감, 91×116.8cm, 2024
'Landscapes beyond time (겁외춘경)' – Hymns of the hills Mixed media on canvas, 91×116.8cm, 2024

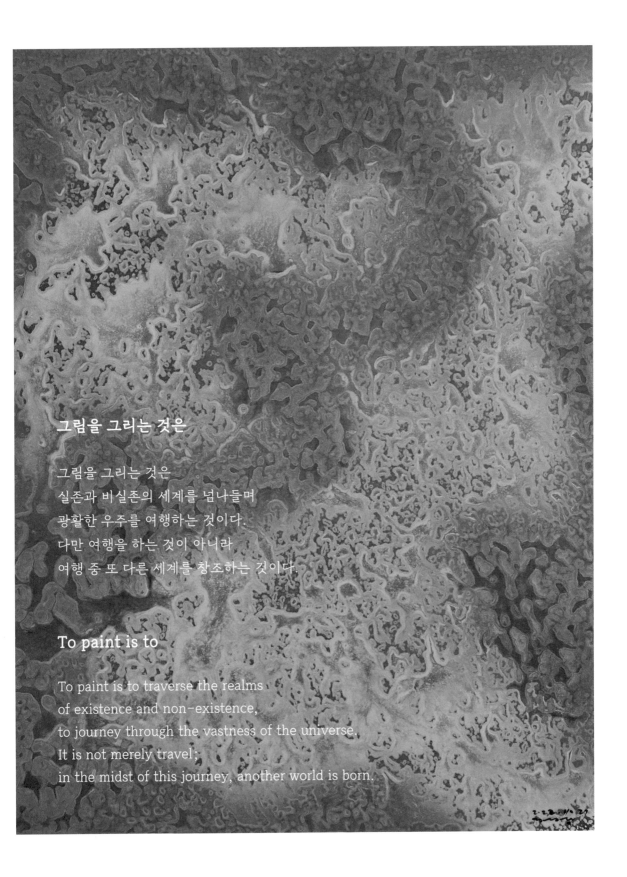

그림을 그리는 것은

그림을 그리는 것은
실존과 비실존의 세계를 넘나들며
광활한 우주를 여행하는 것이다.
다만 여행을 하는 것이 아니라
여행 중 또 다른 세계를 창조하는 것이다.

To paint is to

To paint is to traverse the realms
of existence and non-existence,
to journey through the vastness of the universe.
It is not merely travel;
in the midst of this journey, another world is born.

겁외풍경 - 피오르드 캔버스에 혼합물감, 91×116.8cm, 2023
'Landscapes beyond time (겁외풍경)' – Fjord Mixed media on canvas, 91×116.8cm, 2023

만행(萬行) 화선지에 먹, 21×34cm, 2011
Endless journey (萬行) Ink on rice paper, 21×34cm, 2011

이 눈물 많은 세상

가고 싶다, 세상 어디라도.
이 몸뚱이 천년을 쥐어짜 강을 이루고
억년을 쥐어짜 바다를 이룬다면
그리하여 그대 눈물 닦아 낼 수 있다면
그대 평온할 수 있다면
가고 싶다, 세상 어디라도.
이 눈물 많은 세상
강이 되고 싶다, 바다가 되고 싶다.

In this tear-filled world

I long to go, anywhere in this world,
to squeeze this body for a thousand years,
to form rivers from my essence,
to wring it out for eons to create seas.
If I could then wipe away your tears,
if your heart could find peace,
I wish to go, anywhere in this world,
in this tear-filled existence.
I want to become a river, to become a sea.

부조리

물은 막히면 돌아가고 바람은 막히면 스쳐 간다.
막힘을 뚫고 가려는 것은 오직 인간뿐이다.
세상의 모든 부조리는 여기서 비롯된다.

Absurdity

When water meets an obstacle, it flows around;
when wind is hindered, it whispers past.
Only humans strive to break through barriers,
and from this desire springs all the absurdities of the world.

그림의 힘

감동이 있는 그림은 아무런 설명이 필요 없다.
정말 좋은 그림은 사람이 그림을 이해하기 전에
그림이 먼저 사람을 품어 버린다, 인간의 온갖 분별심을.
그래서 감동이 일어난다.

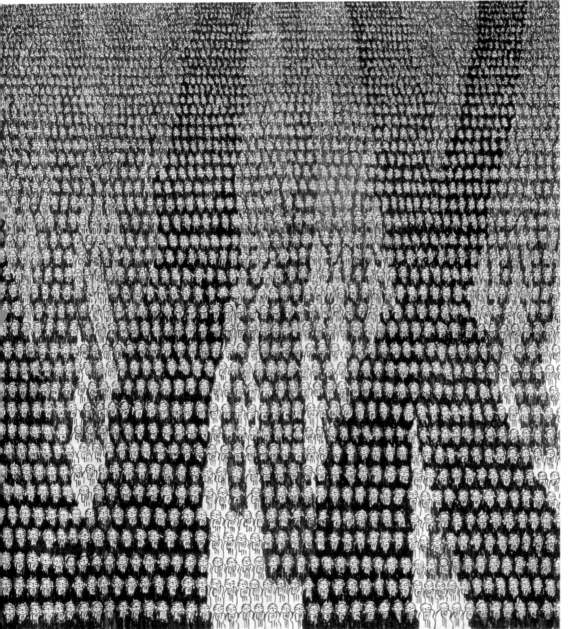

화엄법계도 – 소나무 숲 화성지에 먹 수채화물감, 180×110cm, 2014

Diagram of the Avatamsaka Realm (화엄법계도) – Pine forest Watercolor on rice paper, 180×110cm, 2014

The power of a painting

A painting imbued with emotion needs no words.
A truly great work embraces the viewer,
before they even grasp its meaning.
In this embrace, all human distinctions fade,
and therein lies the spark of inspiration.

참수행자

참수행자는 혼자 노는 법을 안다.
혼자 논다는 것은 매 순간 존재의 느낌대로
전체로 사는 것, 순간이 영원임을 아는 것,
우주와 함께 지금을 노는 것.

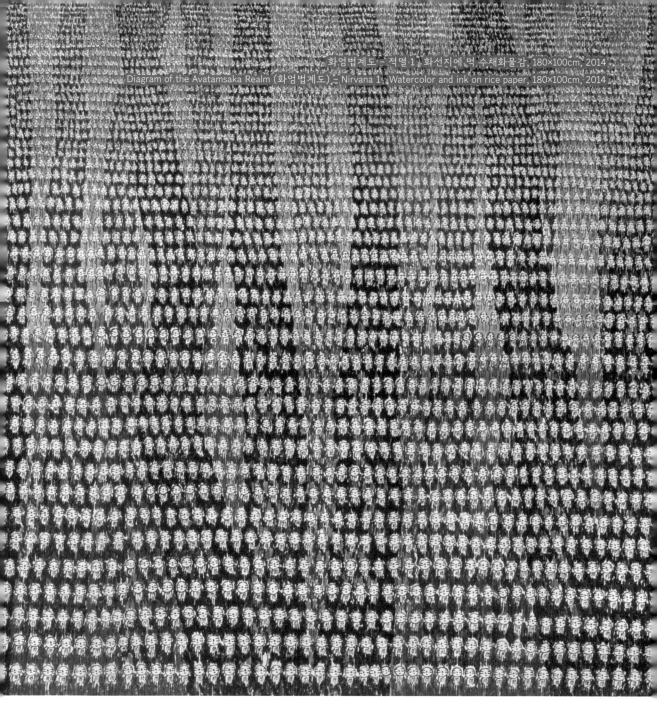

화엄법계도 – 적멸 1, 화선지에 먹 수채화물감, 180×100cm, 2014
Diagram of the Avatamsaka Realm (화엄법계도) – Nirvana 1, Watercolor and ink on rice paper, 180×100cm, 2014

The true practitioner

The true practitioner knows how to play alone.
To play alone is to live fully, feeling each moment of existence,
Recognizing that the present is eternal,
dancing with the universe in this very now.

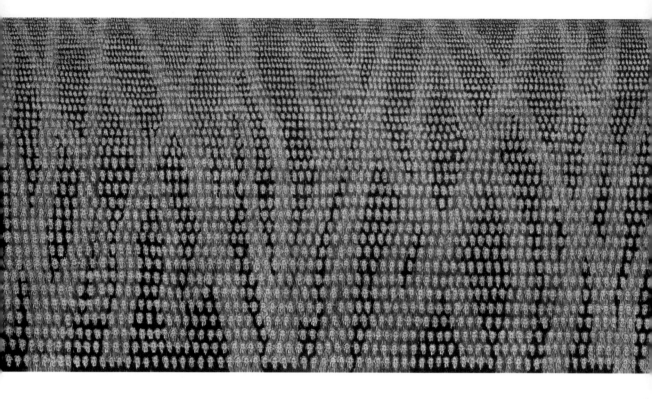

화엄법계도 – 적멸 2 화선지에 먹, 180×110cm, 2014
Diagram of the Avatamsaka Realm (화엄법계도) – Nirvana 2 Ink on rice paper,
180×110cm, 2014

자유인의 영혼

새벽 명상은
우주의 심장에 고요히 홀로 앉는 것이다.
자유인의 영혼은 외로움도 자유, 고독도 자유다.
그에게 외로움은 새의 날개와 같고
고독은 멀리 보는 눈과 같다.

The soul of the free person

Dawn meditation is,
quietly sitting alone at the heart of the universe.
The soul of the free person knows that both loneliness and
solitude are freedom.
To them, loneliness is like the wings of a bird,
and solitude, like the eyes that gaze into the distance.

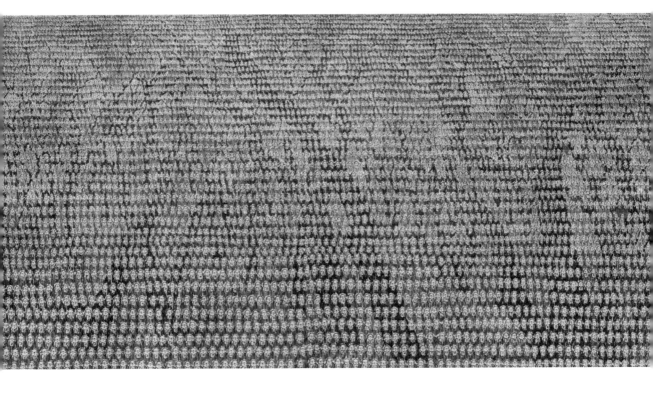

화엄법계도 – 무상 화석지의 및 수채화물감, 180×110cm, 2013
Diagram of the Avatamsaka Realm (화엄법계도) – Impermanence Ink on rice paper,
180×110cm, 2013

고귀한 감정

외로워서 좋다, 고독해서 좋다.
쓸쓸해서 더욱 좋다.
만약 인간에게 이러한 감정이 없었더라면
삶도 인생도 별 의미가 없을 것이다.
오늘 외롭고 고독한 자여!
쓸쓸한 자여!
이 고귀한 감정을 마음껏 즐겨라.

A noble emotion

I rejoice in my loneliness; I cherish my solitude.
The emptiness deepens the joy even more.
If humanity were devoid of such feelings,
life and existence would hold no meaning.
O you who feel lonely today!
O you who are solitary!
Embrace this noble emotion to your heart's content.

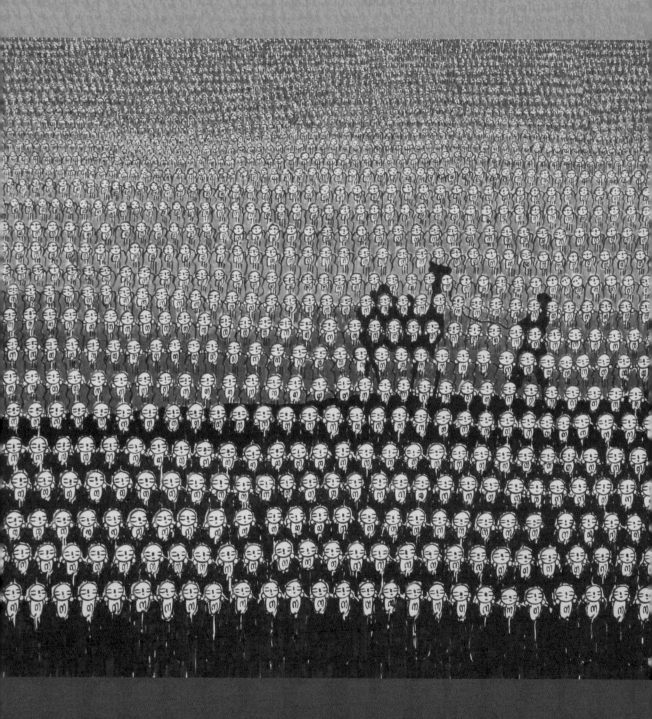

232

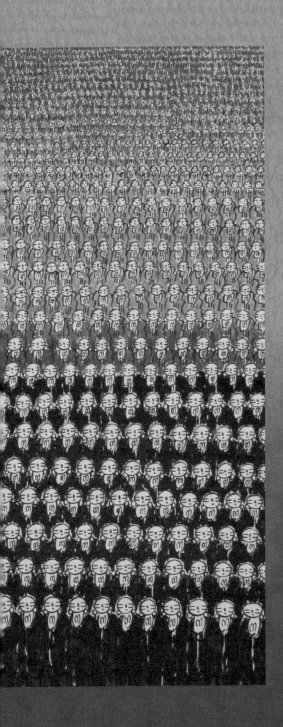

사랑과 자비

초저녁 별이 쓸쓸하다.
어둠 속에 흔들리는 갈대도.
만약 이 세상에 쓸쓸함이 없었다면
무엇으로 세상을 녹이며 살까.
나에게 쓸쓸함은 이 세상 모든 것을 품고
받아들이는 사랑과 자비이다.

Love and compassion

The early evening star is lonely,
and the reeds sway gently in the darkness.
If there were no loneliness in this world,
what would warm our hearts as we live?
For me, loneliness is a love that embraces,
and a compassion that accepts all in this world.

화엄법계도 - 낙타를 모는 성자(비마) 화선지에 수채화물감,
116×80cm, 2013, 인도여행 중 67세의 인도인 할아버지 비마와
사막을 여행하며
Diagram of the Avatamsaka Realm (화엄법계도) – The Sage
guiding the Camel   Watercolor on rice paper, 116×80cm, 2013,
During a trip in India, traveling through the desert with Bima (67
years of age)

붉은 가슴

무슨 일을 시작하면
직성이 풀릴 때까지 해야 한다.
석가의 6년 고행도 직성 풀기 위함이요
깨달음 또한 직성 풀기 위한 것이다.
그림도 마찬가지, 초기 작품 화엄법계도는
어느 정도 직성이 풀렸고
허허당 초실존화도 곧 직성이 풀리리라.
절박하면 보인다. 간절하면 일어난다.
봄날에 새싹 돋듯.

쉬고 싶어도 쉬지 못한 것은
가슴이 하나뿐인 탓이요
놓고 싶어도 놓지 못한 것은
하나뿐인 가슴이 타고 있기에,
붉은 가슴이.

"화엄법계도 – 백만 동자(새벽)"를 그리며

234

화엄법계도 – 백만 동자(새벽) 화선지에 먹, 1120×280cm, 2008
Diagram of the Avatamsaka Realm (화엄법계도) – A Million Young Monks (Dawn) Ink on rice paper, 1120×280cm, 2008

A heart aflame

When embarking on a task,
one must pursue it until the spirit finds ease.
Buddha's six years of asceticism were to release his heart,
and enlightenment, too, is for that same purpose.
Art follows suit;
Early works like 'Avatamsaka Realm' have found their release,
And soon, Huhhuhdang's 'Super-Existentialism' will too.
When desperation strikes, clarity emerges;
When earnestness calls, creation unfolds,
like new shoots breaking forth in spring.

Though I wish to rest, I cannot,
for there is but one heart to bear it all.
Though I long to let go, I cannot,
for that singular heart burns bright;
A heart aflame in crimson.

While painting – "Diagram of the Avatamsaka Realm (화엄법계도) – A Million
Young Monks (Dawn)"

니가 최고야

남미 여행 중 브라질 살바도르 해변가에서
길을 잃고 헤매는 나에게 엄지 척을 날리며
"니가 최고야!" 하고 힘을 실어주었던
두 흑인 소녀의 강렬한 눈빛과 사랑.
영원히 잊을 수 없는 아름다운 추억, 니가 최고야!
오늘 비로소 이 그림을 그린다.

You are the best

During my journey in South America,
On the shores of Salvador, Brazil,
I found myself lost and wandering,
When two girls, with thumbs raised high,
Cheered me on with their fierce gazes,
'You are the best!' Their love a vibrant gift,
An unforgettable memory,
'You are the best!'
Today, at last, I paint this picture.

니가 최고야 화선지에 먹, 36×51cm, 2005
You are the best   Ink on rice paper, 36×51cm, 2005

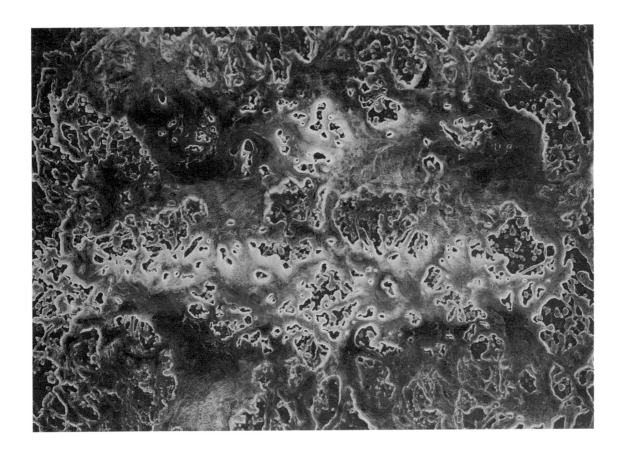

겁외풍경 - 고요한 기쁨 캔버스에 혼합물감, 80.3×116.8cm, 2023
'Landscapes beyond time (겁외풍경)' - Tranquil Happiness
Mixed media on canvas, 80.3×116.8cm, 2023

한 점 바람처럼

즐겁게 놀아라. 삶도 죽음도 노는 것이다.
우리가 이 세상에 온 것은
한 점 바람처럼 가볍게 놀다 가기 위함이다.
깨달음이란 이 도리를 알고
한세상 가볍게 노는 것이다.

Like a whisper of the wind

Rejoice and frolic, for both life and death are but a dance.
We have come to this world
to frolic lightly, like a whisper of the wind.
Enlightenment lies in knowing this truth,
in embracing a life of joyous frolics.

허허당 초실존화

허허당 초실존화는 붓이 캔버스에 닿지 않고 그리는 그림이다. 이 방법을
연구한 것은 7년 전으로, 그동안 그려온 화엄법계도와 개미, 새 등 아주 세밀한
그림들을 그리면서 목디스크와 어지럼증으로 인해 한동안 그림을 그릴 수가
없어, 화엄법계도처럼 극도로 몰입하지 않고도 그림을 그릴 수 있는 방법을
찾은 것이 허허당 초실존화다. 초실존화는 모든 실존세계를 부정한 후에 오는
것이기에 논리적 모순이 생기지 않을 수 없다. 그러나 그림을 그리는 순간
일체 생명이 하나의 모습으로 분명히 실존하는 것을 경험하게 된다.

Huhuhdang's 'Super-Existentialism'

Huhuhdang's 'Super-Existentialism' is a painting created without the
brush touching the canvas. This method was developed seven years ago,
during a time when I could not paint due to cervical disc issues and
dizziness, after having worked on intricate pieces like the 'Huayombeopgye' and detailed images of ants and birds. I sought a way to
create art without the extreme immersion required for works like the
'Huayombeopgye.' 'Super-Existentialism' arises after rejecting all
existential realities, which inevitably leads to logical contradictions. Yet,
in the moment of painting, one experiences the profound truth that all
life exists as a singular form.

겁외풍경 – 씨줄 날줄 캔버스에 혼합물감, 65.1×91cm, 2022, 2023
'Landscapes beyond time (겁외풍경)' – Theads of Life   Mixed media on canvas, 65.1×91cm, 2022, 2023

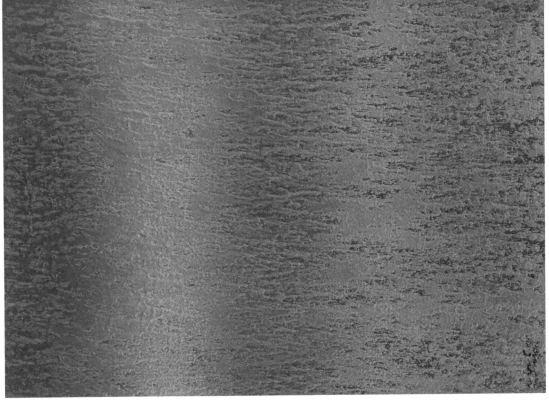

239

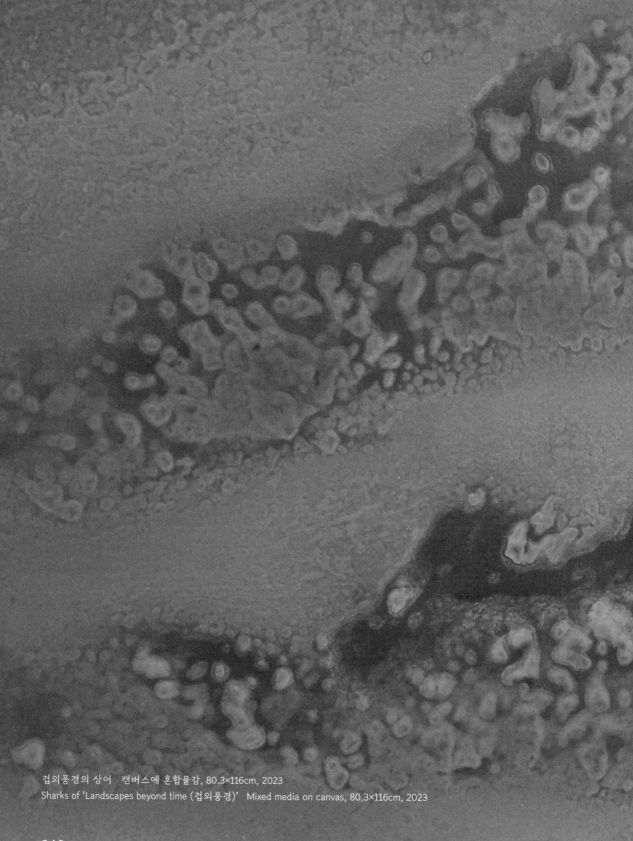

겹외풍경의 상어   캔버스에 혼합물감, 80.3×116cm, 2023
Sharks of 'Landscapes beyond time (겹외풍경)'   Mixed media on canvas, 80.3×116cm, 2023

눈 깜짝할 사이

세상을 잠시 휴가 나온 기분으로 살면 어떨까?
그런 기분으로 산다고 해서 뭐라 하는 사람은 없을 것이다.
그렇다고 긴 휴가도 아니다. 눈 깜짝할 사이다.
인생을 잠시 휴가 나온 기분으로 살면 어디를 가도 마음이 설레고
누구를 만나도 잘해 주고 싶다. 순간순간 낯선 휴가지에서
만난 사람들이기에 늘 새롭고 설레인다.

A blink of an eye

What if, we lived as if we were on a brief holiday?
No one would question such a feeling,
though it's not a long vacation, just a blink of an eye.
Living life as if on a fleeting retreat,
every destination sparks joy,
and every encounter inspires kindness.
In each moment, strangers become fresh faces,
filling the heart with wonder and delight.

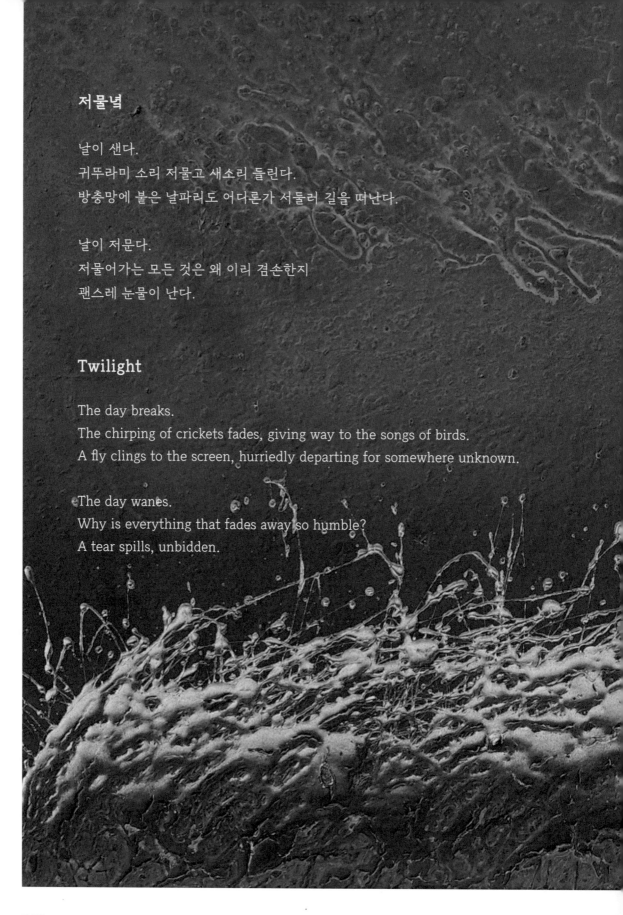

저물녘

날이 샌다.
귀뚜라미 소리 저물고 새소리 들린다.
방충망에 붙은 날파리도 어디론가 서둘러 길을 떠난다.

날이 저문다.
저물어가는 모든 것은 왜 이리 겸손한지
괜스레 눈물이 난다.

Twilight

The day breaks.
The chirping of crickets fades, giving way to the songs of birds.
A fly clings to the screen, hurriedly departing for somewhere unknown.

The day wanes.
Why is everything that fades away so humble?
A tear spills, unbidden.

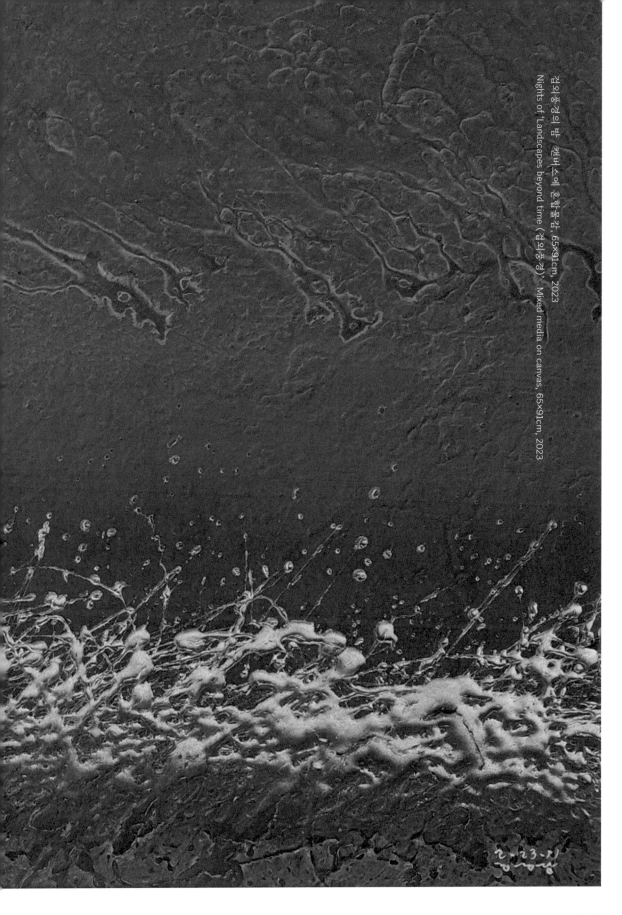

겹의풍경의 밤 캔버스에 혼합물감 65×91cm, 2023

Nights of 'Landscapes beyond time (겹의풍경)' Mixed media on canvas, 65×91cm, 2023

겹외풍경의 금붕어 캔버스에 혼합물감, 100×80.3cm, 2023
Goldfish of 'Landscapes beyond time (겹외풍경)' Mixed media on canvas, 100×80.3cm, 2023

244

산중의 하루

이슬 먹은 풀들이 고요하다. 아직 날개를 털지 못한 새들도 소리가 없고 무주공산 텅 빈 계곡만 잠 깨어 있다. 길 건너 노란 꽃이 말했다. 움직이는 모든 것은 아름답다. 산 빛이 꽃말에 꼬리를 달았다. 혹은 더럽거나 치사하다. 마당을 쓸고 빨래를 한다.

아침에 보았던 길 건너 노란 꽃이 오후엔 약간 방향을 바꾸어 계곡을 품고 있는 갈대밭으로 고개를 숙였다. 바람이 아래서 위로 불 땐 갈대가 꽃잎을 어루만지고 위에서 아래로 불 땐 노란 꽃이 갈대를 어루만지며 엇갈린 바람의 길을 따라 서로 다정하게 사랑을 속삭인다.

장마가 끝나고 바위틈 사이 덩그러니 고인 물은 본성대로 흐르길 갈망하나 좀처럼 흐르지 못해 비틀거린다. 물살 위에 미세한 생명들이 제 존재의 여부를 알리느라 퐁퐁 바쁘다. 여치, 날파리, 풍뎅이, 하루살이. 해가 저문다.

A day in the mountains

The dew-kissed grass lies in silence. Even the fledgling birds hold their voices, and only the empty valley stirs awake. Across the road, the yellow flower speaks: "Everything that moves is beautiful." The mountain light trails behind its petals, or perhaps it is sullied and trivial. I sweep the yard and hang the laundry.

The yellow flower I saw in the morning turns slightly in the afternoon, bowing to the reeds embracing the valley. When the wind blows from below, the reeds caress the petals, and when it flows from above, the yellow flower tenderly touches the reeds, whispering love along the path of intertwining breezes.

After the rains, the water pooled between the rocks longs to flow, but it struggles, twisting in its stillness. Tiny lives atop the current, busily declaring their existence: crickets, flies, beetles, and mayflies as the sun dips below the horizon.

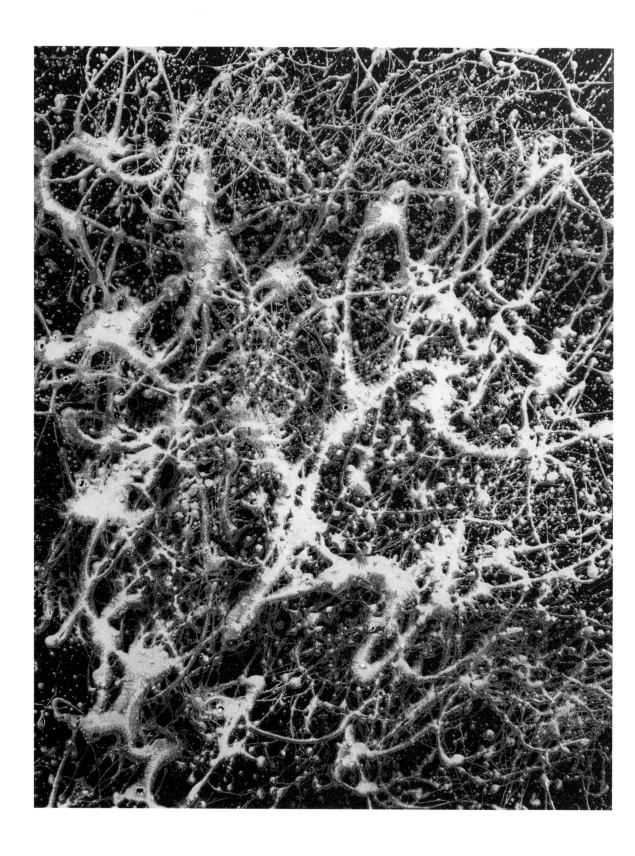

누릴 줄 알아야

세상에 있는 그 어떤 것도
가지기 위해 있는 것이 아니라
누리기 위해 있는 것이다.

세상을 가지기 위해 사는 사람은
아무리 가져도 허망하고
누리기 위해 사는 사람은
매 순간 있는 그대로 행복하다.

To know how to embrace

Nothing in this world exists
to be possessed; it exists to be embraced.

Those who live to possess the world find emptiness in all they grasp,
while those who live to savor life find joy in simply being.

겁외풍경 - 눈꽃축제 캔버스에 혼합물감, 80.2×100cm, 2022
'Landscapes beyond time (겁외풍경)' – Snow Blossom Festival Mixed media on canvas, 80.2×100cm, 2022

콩닥거리는 가슴

자운영!
나는 아직 꽃 이름 중에
이보다 예쁜 이름을 알지 못한다.
자주색 꽃망울을 터트리는 자운영의 자태는
첫사랑이 눈뜨는 마음이다.
자운영은 콩닥거리는 가슴만이
볼 수 있다.

A fluttering heart

'Jaeun-Young!'
I have yet to discover a name more beautiful
than yours among all the flowers.
The splendor of your violet buds bursting open
is the awakening heart of first love.
Only a fluttering heart
can truly behold 'Jaeun-Young.'

겹외풍경 – 줄기세포 캔버스에 혼합물감, 91×116.8cm, 2022
'Landscapes beyond time (겹외풍경)' – Stem Cells Mixed media on canvas, 91×116.8cm, 2022

눈 깜짝할 새 화선지에 수채화물감, 32×35cm, 2011
A Blink of an eye Watercolor on rice paper, 32×35cm, 2011

존재의 울림

사람과 사람 사이
단 한 번의 만남으로도 영원한 것이 있다.
존재의 울림!
정신적 교감은 멀고 가까움이 없다.
진정한 사랑은
단 한 번의 만남으로도 영원하다.

The resonance of existence

Between one soul and another,
even a single meeting can birth the eternal.
The resonance of existence!
In spiritual connection, distance dissolves.
True love, with just one encounter,
becomes everlasting.

참자유인

참자유인은 홀로 심심할 줄 안다.
인간의 창의성은 고요히 홀로 있을 때 찾아온다.
그것이 무엇이든
고독, 외로움 혹은 고통일지라도.

The truly free soul

Truly free souls know the art of solitary serenity.
In quietude, creativity finds its genesis.
Be it solitude, loneliness, or even pain's intensity.
Human ingenuity blooms in stillness.

진심

지혜로운 자는
밭을 일구고 씨 뿌리며 인생을 깨닫고
땀 흘리며 행복을 노래한다.
사람이 만든 과실 중에 피와 땀,
진심이 서려 있지 않은 것은
열매를 맺어도 썩어버린다.
무엇이든 부정한 방법으로 얻은 것은
세상을 이롭게 하지 못한다.

Sincerity

The wise cultivate the fields and sow their seeds,
embracing the lessons of life,
singing of happiness through their toil.
Among the fruits crafted by human hands,
those lacking blood, sweat, and sincerity
will rot, even if they bear fruit.
Anything gained through dishonest means
brings no benefit to the world.

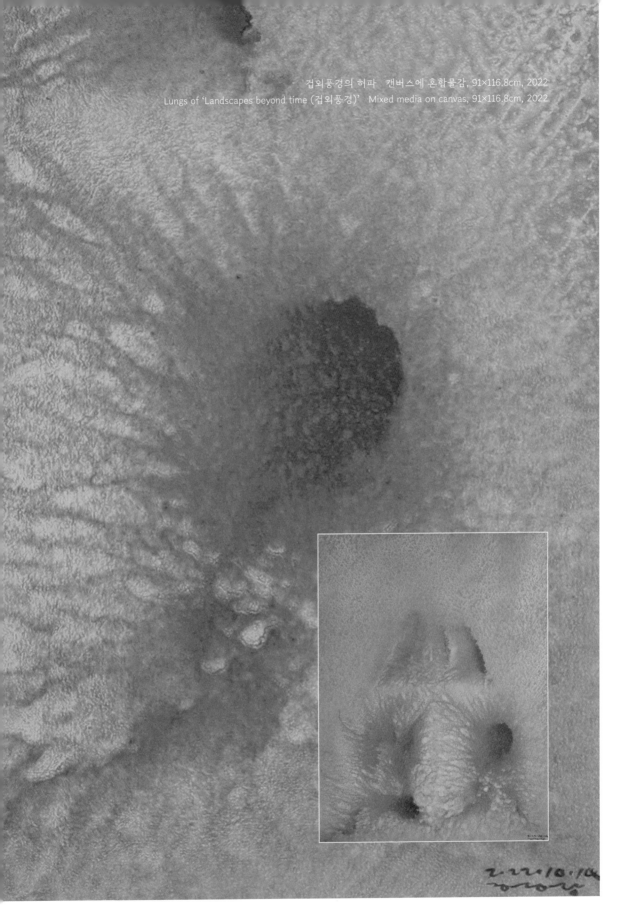

겁외풍경의 허파 캔버스에 혼합물감, 91×116.8cm, 2022
Lungs of 'Landscapes beyond time (겁외풍경)' Mixed media on canvas, 91×116.8cm, 2022

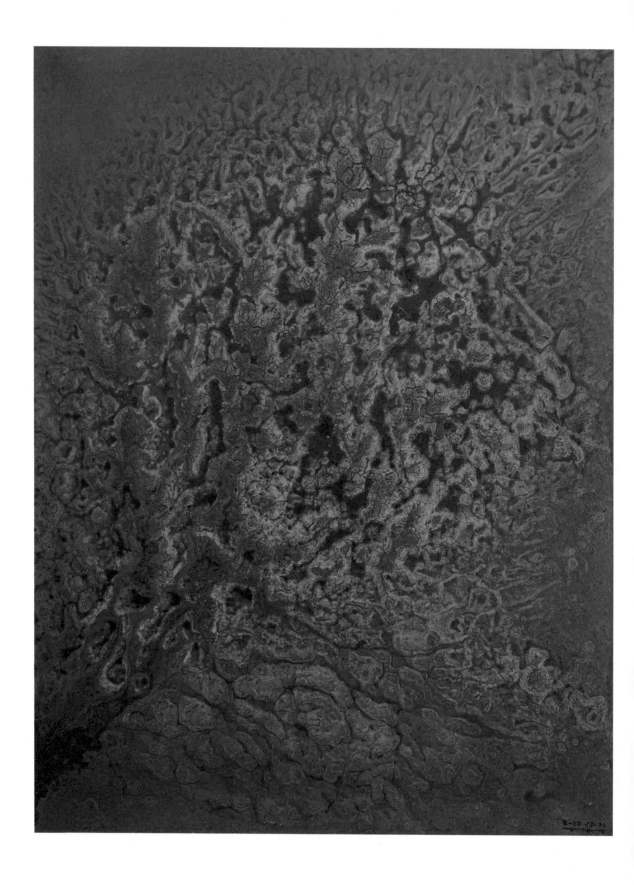

시의 몸

한 수의 시를 쓴다는 것은 한 번의 죽음을 의미하고
한 장의 그림을 그린다는 것은 한 번의 화장을 의미한다.
참으로 죽지 않는 예술은 예술일 수가 없다.
진정한 예술은 반드시 죽음을 선택한다.

시는 어떻게 쓰는가? 손, 머리, 의식, 아니다.
시를 쓰는 것은 몸이다. 그러나 몸은 시를 쓰지 않는다.
몸은 죽어 환생한다, 시의 몸으로.
진정 살아 있는 시는 몸과 시를 맞바꾼다.

A poem's body

To write a line of poetry is to embrace a death,
and to create a canvas is to undergo a transformation.
True art, untouched by death, cannot truly exist.
Genuine artistry must choose death as its companion.

How does one craft a poem? It's not mere hand or thought.
To write is to embody, yet the body does not write.
The body dies and is reborn,
becoming the essence of poetry.
In this way, a living poem exchanges its body for the soul of verse.

겁외풍경의 뇌 캔버스에 혼합물감, 91×116.8cm, 2022
The Brain of 'Landscapes beyond time (겁외풍경)' Mixed media on canvas, 91×116.8cm, 2022

전설과 신화

전설과 신화는
인간의 힘이 미치지 못한 것들을
다른 무엇에 의해 실현하고자 했던
인간의 상상력에서 비롯된 것이지만
그것 자체로 아름답다.

Legends and myths

Legends and myths arise
from the imagination of humanity,
yearning to realize what is beyond our grasp.
Yet, in their essence,
they hold a beauty all their own,
a testament to dreams unbound by reality.

겁외풍경 – 전설의 바다 캔버스에 혼합물감, 116.8×91cm, 2023
'Landscapes beyond time 〈겁외풍경〉' – The Ocean of Myths Mixed media on canvas, 116.8×91cm, 2023

선재동자 화선지에 수채화물감, 31×35cm, 2011
The Bodhisattva of Samantabhadra Watercolor on rice paper, 31×35cm, 2011

스스로 길임을 아는 것은

길은 길을 묻지 않고 길은 길을 가지 않네.
스스로 길임을 아는 것은
아무런 길도 묻지 않고 아무런 길도 가지 않네.
오직 사람만이 길을 묻고 길을 가는 것은
인간은 만물의 영장이라는 착각 속에서
길을 잃었기 때문이리.
자기를 겸손히 살피는 자 만물이 스스로 길이 되네.

To recognize oneself as the path

The path asks not for directions, nor does it journey forth.
To recognize oneself as the path is to seek no guidance,
to tread no road.
Only humans inquire and wander,
lost in the illusion of being the crown of creation.
Yet those who humbly reflect on themselves
find that all beings become the way.

물기 있게 살다 가자

물기 있게 살다 물기 있게 죽자.
단풍잎도 물기 있는 것은 붉고 아름답게 떨어지고
물기 없는 것은 푸석하니 쓸쓸히 떨어지더라.
인간에게 물기란 따뜻한 정 아니겠느냐.
정답게 살다 정답게 죽자.
물기 있게.

Let us live and die with moisture

Let us live with moisture, and let us die with moisture.
Even maple leaves that are dewy fall red and beautiful,
while the dry ones drop with a lonely whisper.
For humanity, moisture is warmth and tenderness, is it not?
Let us live tenderly and die tenderly,
in this embrace of moisture.

접외풍경의 꽃비 캔버스에 혼합물감, 80.3×116cm, 2022
Flower Rains of 'Landscapes beyond time (접외풍경)' Mixed media on canvas, 80.3×116cm, 2022

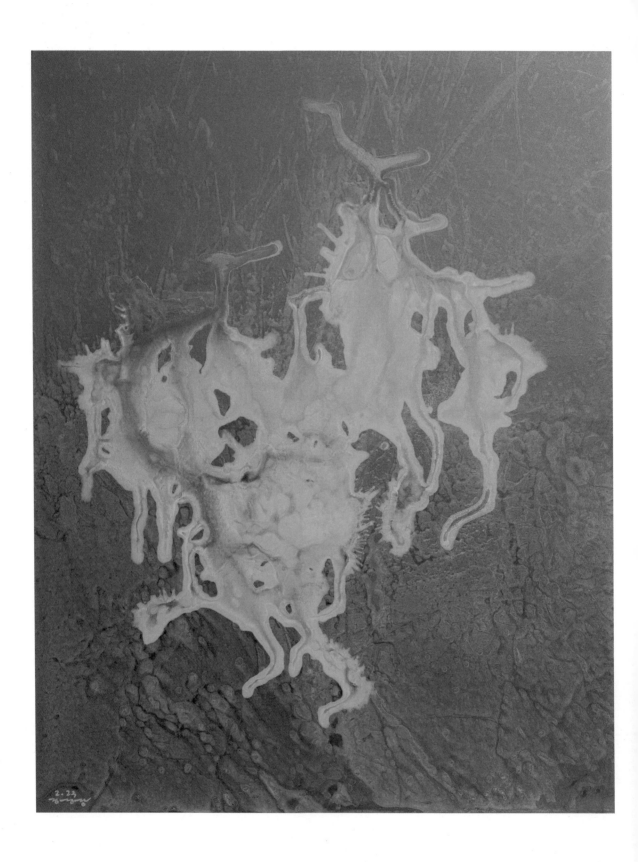

무심히 보고 듣는 것

보라 해서 보는 것과 들으라 해서 듣는 것은
아무리 애써 보고 애써 들어도 큰 감흥이 없고
무심히 보고 듣는 것은 그 자체로 놀라움이다.
애써 보고 들을 게 없으면
절로 보이고 절로 들린다.

To observe and listen with a careless heart

To see because one is told to see, and to hear because one is told to hear,
no matter how hard one tries, it stirs little within.
Yet to observe and listen with a careless heart brings forth the wonder in itself.
When there's nothing to forcefully seek,
vision and sound emerge effortlessly, revealing their own magic.

겹외풍경 – 사슴과 새   캔버스에 혼합물감, 80.3×100cm, 2023
'Landscapes beyond time (겹외풍경)' – A deer and a bird   Mixed media on canvas, 80.3×100cm, 2023

꽃피고 꽃 진다

삶은 매 순간 기적이다.
바람 불고 낙엽 지고 꽃피고 지고
세상사 모든 것 기적 아닌 게 있더냐.
보라! 그대의 삶이 기적이다.
존재 그 자체로.

The blooming and fading of a flower

Life is a miracle in every moment.
The wind blows, leaves fall, flowers bloom and fade.
Is there anything in this world that isn't miraculous?
Behold! Your life is a miracle,
Simply by existing.

우주와 일대일로 맞선 개미 화선지에 수채화물감, 31×35cm, 2011
An Ant Confronting the Universe Watercolor on rice paper, 31×35cm, 2011

진정한 아름다움

하루 한 시간 혹은 두 시간 정도
고요히 자신을 지켜보는 시간을 갖는다면
자신이 참 아름다운 사람임을 안다.
고요 속엔 모든 것을 아름답게 볼 수 있는 눈이 열린다.
세상이 아무리 아름답다 해도
그대 자신의 아름다움을 발견하는 것만 못하다.

True beauty

If you take an hour or two each day
to quietly observe yourself,
you'll realize just how beautiful you truly are.
In that stillness, eyes open to beauty in all things.
No matter how lovely the world may seem,
discovering your own beauty is the greatest revelation.

겹외풍경 – 사리셀카의 숲   캔버스에 혼합물감, 91×116.8cm, 2022, 북유럽 여행 중 핀란드 사리셀카에서
'Landscapes beyond time (겹외풍경)' – Forests of Sariselka   Mixed media on canvas, 91×116.8cm, 2022,
During a trip in Scandinavia, Sarisellka, Finland

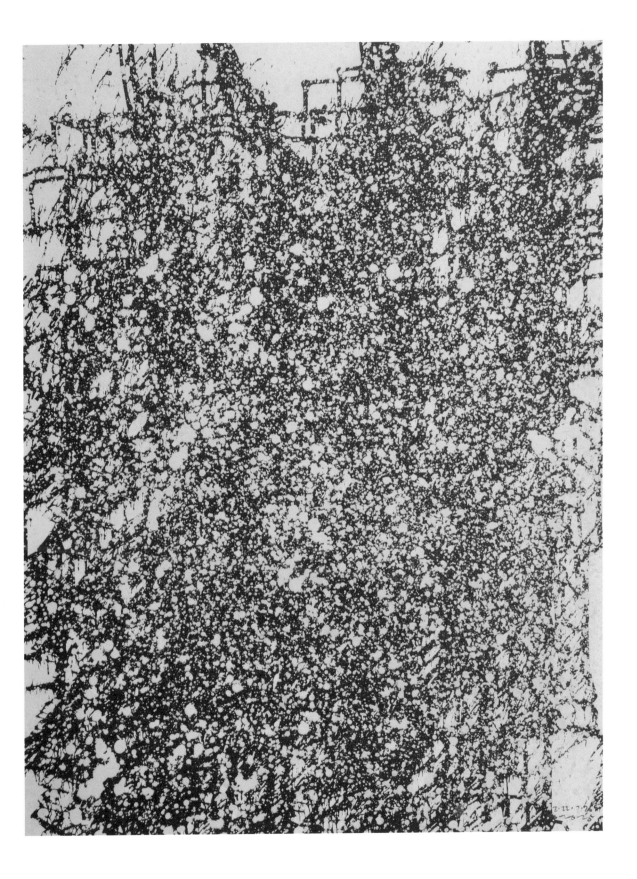

겨울새

겨울 아침에 보는 새는 참 반갑기도 하다.
짹- 얼음이 깨어지듯 깨끗한 소리.
눈은 또 얼마나 초롱한지.
새 한 마리가 온 세상을 품고 있다.

Winterbird

On a winter morning, a bird is truly a welcome sight,
Its chirp, crisp as ice breaking, fills the air with pure delight.
How bright its eyes, sparkling like the morning dew,
a single bird cradles the whole world in its view.

겸외풍경 – 역결세포 캔버스에 혼합물감, 91×116.8cm, 2022
'Landscapes beyond time (겸외풍경)' – Intertwined Cells Mixed media on canvas, 91×116.8cm, 2022

우주는 하나의 큰 생명 덩어리

산중의 밤은 겨울이다.
하늘에도 세포가 있고 바람에도 비에도 세포가 있다.
우주는 하나의 큰 생명 덩어리.
이 모든 세포들은 하나로 연결되어 있다.

The universe is a vast being

The night in the mountains is winter's embrace.
Cells dwell in the sky, in the winds, in the rains.
The universe is a vast being,
And all these cells are intertwined as one.

선승의 눈 – 사자후 캔버스에 먹, 91×116.8cm, 2023
The Eyes of the Zen Master – The Lion's Roar Ink on canvas, 91×116.8cm, 2023

거짓 없는 세계

눈으로 보는 것은 더 볼 게 없어야 보이고
마음으로 보는 것은 더 알 게 없어야 보인다.
진실로 거짓 없는 세계를 마주하려면.

A world free of deceit

To see with the eyes, one must have no desire for more,
To see with the heart, one must seek no further understanding.
To truly confront a world free of deceit, one must embrace the simplicity of being.

그림 속에 나타난 새들이 밤새 물소리 듣는다.
오호, 난 너의 포로가 되고 넌 소리의 포로가 되었구나.

The birds within the painting listen to the water's whisper through the night.
Oh, how I've become your captive, and you, the captive of sound.

겹외풍경 – 숲의 노래 캔버스에 먹, 91×116.8cm, 2022
'Landscapes beyond time (겹외풍경)' – Hymns of the Forest Ink on canvas, 91×116.8cm, 2022

그림 그리는 마음

목성과 화성에 나무를 심었다.
언젠가 지구에 인간이 살 수 없을 때가 오면
목성과 화성에 인간이 살 수 있길 바라며

The heart that paints

I have planted trees on Jupiter and Mars,
hoping that when the time comes,
and Earth no longer holds humanity,
these distant worlds may cradle our kind

화성에 심은 나무 캔버스에 먹, 91×65.2cm, 2022

Trees planted on Mars Ink on canvas, 91×65.2cm, 2022

청동 미소

물살에 흔들리는 달빛을 바라보다
바짓가랑이 다 젖는 줄 몰랐다.
물밑 잔돌멩이들의 청동빛 미소
억겁의 세월을 고스란히 담고 있다.
왼발을 드니 엄지발가락에 끼인
청동 미소가 온 산을 웃게 한다.

A bronze smile

Gazing at the moonlight trembling on the water's flow,
I didn't realize my pant legs were soaked.
Beneath the surface, the smooth stones wear
a bronze smile, holding the ages within.
As I lift my left foot, a smile ensnared
on my big toe brings laughter to the mountains.

겁외풍경 – 킬리만자로의 숲   캔버스에 먹, 80.3×116cm, 2022, 아프리카 여행 중
'Landscapes beyond time (겁외풍경)' – Forests of Kilimanjaro
Ink on canvas, 80.3×116cm, 2022, During a trip in Africa

겹외풍경 – 생명의 춤   캔버스에 혼합물감, 116.8×80.3cm, 2023
'Landscapes beyond time (겹외풍경)' – Dances of Life
Mixed media on canvas, 116.8×80.3cm, 2023

뽕잎

오후 산책길에 뽕잎 하나 땄다.
뻐꾸기 소리 가득 배인 책갈피에 두면
종일 뻐꾸기 소리 나겠네.

Mulberry leaf

On my afternoon stroll, I plucked a mulberry leaf.
If I place it on the bookmark, soaked in cuckoo calls,
All day long, the cuckoo's song will linger.

274

밤에 우는 새　화선지에 먹, 27×24cm, 2009
The Nightingale's Lament　Ink on rice paper, 27×24cm, 2009

어리석은 자는 좋은 것을 보면 금방 탐하고
현명한 자는 그냥 놓고 보고
지혜로운 자는 얼른 떠난다.

The foolish rush to grasp the good they see,
while the wise observe and let it be,
yet the truly wise know when to depart,
finding beauty in the art of a gentle heart.

농담 화선지에 먹, 31x24cm, 2005
Jests Ink on rice paper, 31x24cm, 2005

농담을 잃어버린 시대

세상을 아름답게 하는 것은 농담이다.
농담을 모르는 사회는 모든 생명 활동을 긴장되게 한다.
농담을 잃어버린 시대, 얼마나 불행한가?
모두 갑옷 입은 전사 같다.

A time that has lost its sense of humor

What Beautifies the World Is a Jest.
A society that knows not laughter tightens the tension of all living things.
How unfortunate is a time that has lost its sense of humor!
Everyone seems a warrior clad in armor.

비상 화선지에 먹, 52×34cm, 2009
Tranquil suicide Ink on rice paper, 52×34cm, 2009

고요한 자살

그림을 그린다는 것은
그리기보다는 품는 것, 닭이 알을 품듯.
존재의 내밀한 그 무엇을 끊임없이 품고 사는 일.
그림을 그린다는 것은
지금의 내가 또 다른 나를 향해
고요한 자살을 꿈꾸는 일.

Tranquil suicide

To paint is not merely to draw,
but to embrace, like a hen brooding over its eggs,
it is a constant nurturing of something profound within existence.
To paint is to dream of,
as the present self reaches toward another self.
a tranquil suicide.

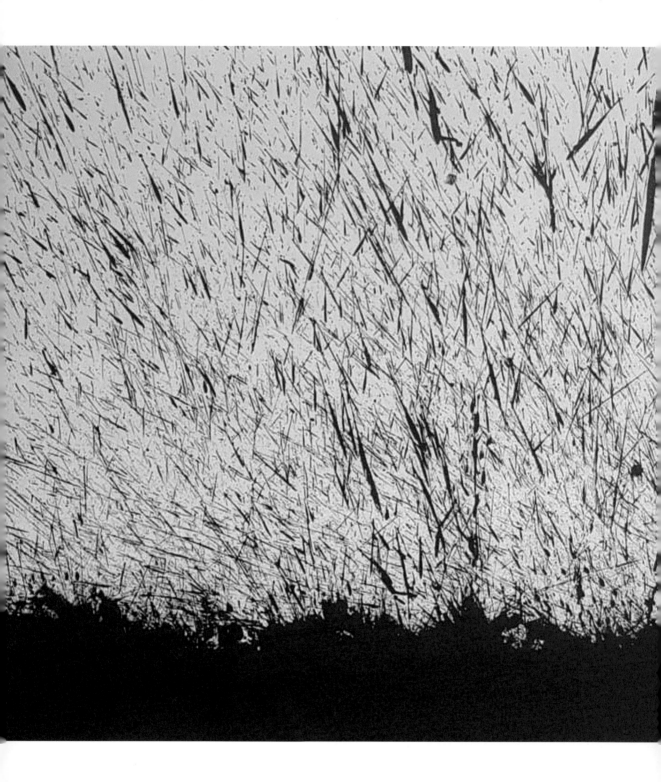

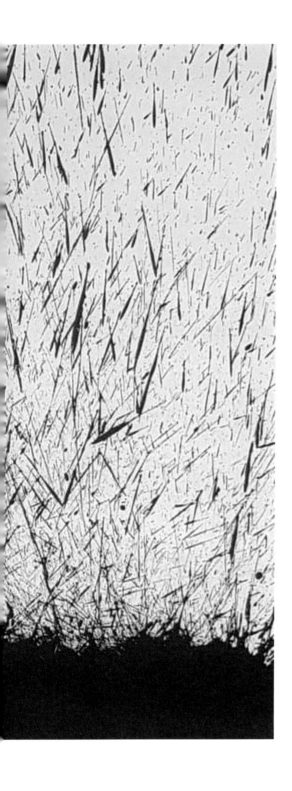

수행자의 삶

수행자는
세상 모든 것이 자신을 향해 박수갈채를 보내도
결코 그 칭찬 속에 머물지 않고
비난을 해도 그 비난 속에 머물지 않는다.
마치 푸른 나뭇가지가 허공을 향해 뻗어 가듯
자신을 향해 뻗어 간다.

The practitioner's life

The practitioner,
though the world may applaud with fervor,
stays not in the embrace of praise;
and when faced with scorn,
does not linger there either.
Like green branches stretching toward the sky,
they reach ever inward, toward their true self.

겁외풍경 - 바람 부는 길섶 캔버스에 먹, 119×80.3cm, 2023
'Landscapes beyond time (겁외풍경)' - By the wind-swept pathside
Ink on canvas, 119×80.3cm, 2023

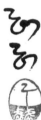

선화는 작가 의지를 통해 그려지는 것이 아니라
무심을 통해 일어나는 것이며 그 일어남을 다만 함께하는 것이다.

선화를 음악적으로 보면 재즈와 같고 화엄법계도는 클래식과 같다.
그리고 겁외풍경은 재즈 블루스다.

수행에 비유하면 선화는 돈오돈수요 화엄법계도는 돈오점수다.
그리고 겁외풍경은 이 모든 것을 품고 노는 것이다.

'Seonhwa (Zen painting)' emerges not from the artist's will,
but through a quiet awareness, simply sharing in its unfolding.

If viewed musically, 'Seonhwa' resembles jazz,
while 'Diagram of the Avatamsaka Realm (화엄법계도)' is classical,
and 'Landscapes beyond time (겁외풍경)' embodies jazz blues.

In the realm of practice, 'Seonhwa' is sudden awakening and gradual
realization (돈오돈수), 'Diagram of the Avatamsaka Realm (화엄법계도)'
reflects the sudden insight (돈오점수), and 'Landscapes beyond time
(겁외풍경)' is where all of this is embraced and played with.

사무침 화선지에 먹, 21×34cm, 2001
Transcendence Ink on rice paper, 21×34cm, 2001

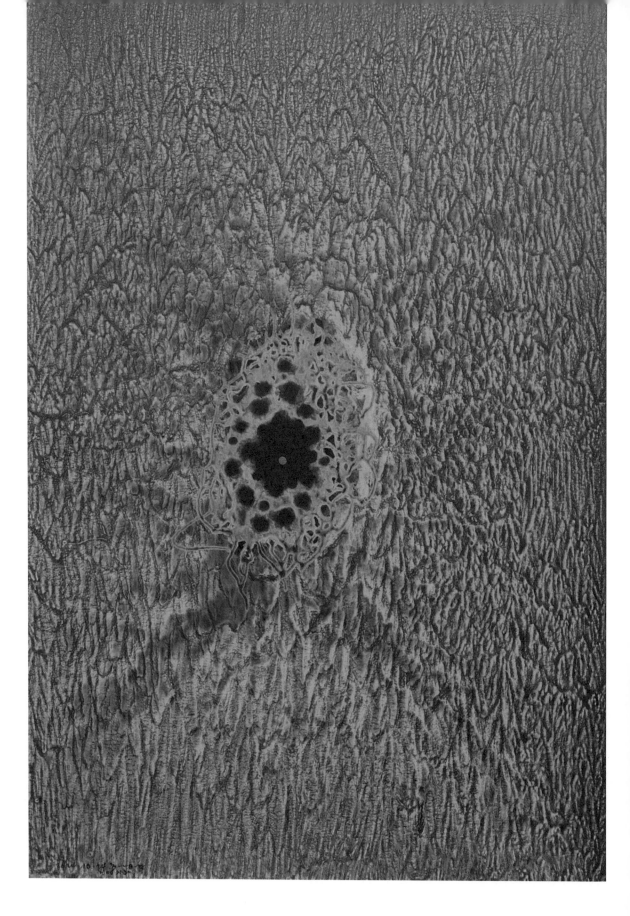

겁외풍경의 노래는 나의 저서 『머물지 마라 그 아픈 상처에』와 『바람에게 길을 물으니 네 멋대로 가라 한다』 외 다수의 작품 중에 일부 좋은 글을 발췌하고 새로 쓴 시와 작품들로 세상 모든 사람들의 가슴속에 하나의 미술관을 짓는 마음으로 정성을 기울였다.

이 한 권의 책, 『겁외풍경의 노래』가 외롭고 힘든 사람들에게는 위로가 되고, 절망에 빠진 사람들에게는 용기가 되고, 실의와 허무에 빠진 사람들에게는 기쁨이 될 수 있는 세상 사람들의 다정한 벗이 되길 염원한다. 그림은 글과 연관성 없이 자유롭게 감상할 수 있도록 했다.

The Hymns of 'Landscapes beyond time (겁외풍경)' are a collection that includes excerpts from my works 'Do Not Dwell on That Painful Wound' and 'When I Ask the Wind for Direction, It Tells Me to Go as I Please,' along with newly written poems and pieces.

I poured my heart into this book with the intention of building a gallery in the hearts of all people and gifting it to them. I hope this one book, 'Landscapes beyond time (겁외풍경)' can provide comfort to those who are lonely and struggling, courage to those who are in despair, and joy to those who feel emptiness, becoming a true companion for the people of this warm world. The illustration of artworks are intended to be viewed freely, without direct relation to the text.

겁외풍경 – 천언지화(하늘 언어 땅의 말) 캔버스에 혼합물감, 80.3×116cm, 2024
'Landscapes beyond time (겁외풍경)' – 천언지화 (Language of the sky, Words of the Earth)
Mixed media on canvas, 80.3×116cm, 2024

겁외풍경 – 활구지언(살아 있는 땅의 언어) 캔버스에 혼합물감, 80.3×116.8cm, 2024
'Landscapes beyond time (겁외풍경)' – 활구지언 (Words of the living Earth)
Mixed media on canvas, 80.3×116.8cm, 2024

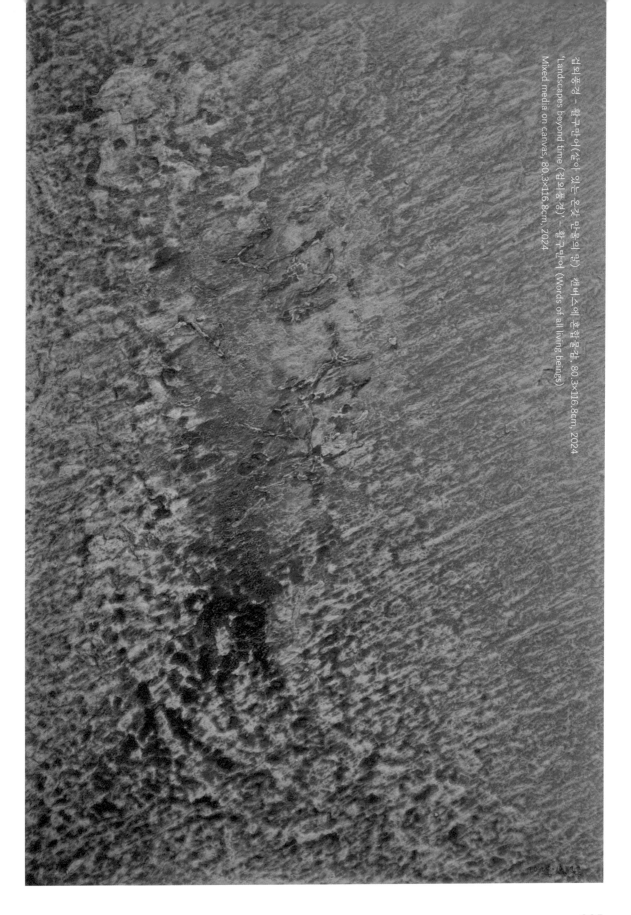

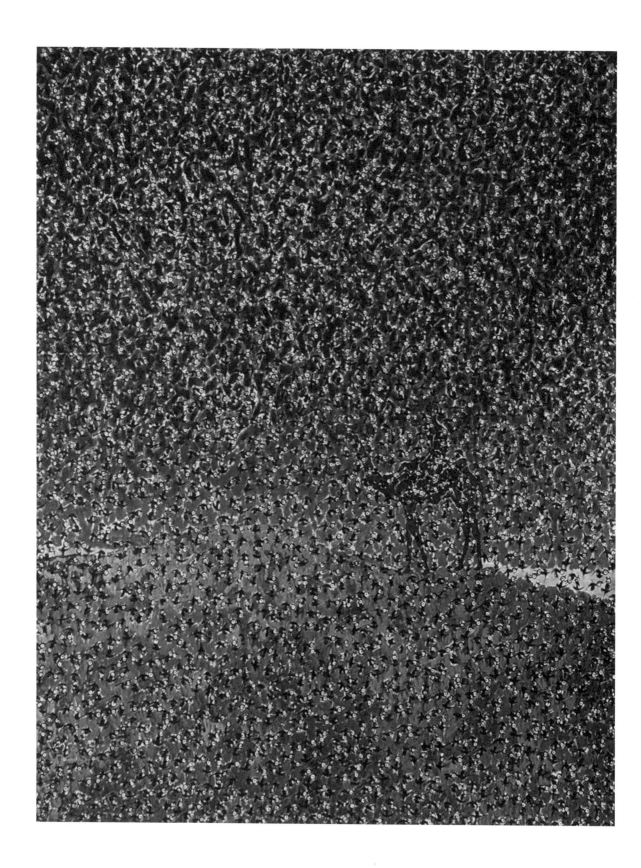

깃털처럼 가볍게

인생의 황혼에는 낙타를 타고 사막을 걷자.
붉게 타오르는 노을빛에 얼굴을 묻고
깃털처럼 가볍게 이승을 날자.
인생의 황혼에는 사막에서 부는 모래바람을 맞으며
인생사 모든 고뇌를 씻고 붉게 쓰러지는 노을빛처럼
환하게 이승을 내려놓자.

As light as a feather

At the twilight of life, let us ride a camel through the desert.
buried in the crimson glow of the setting sun.
Let us soar lightly through this world like feathers.
In life's dusk, as the desert winds sweep across the sands,
let us wash away all the anguish of existence,
and, like the brilliant hues of the sinking sun,
lay down our burdens with grace.

허허당

저서

『머물지 마라 그 아픈 상처에』(위즈덤하우스)

『바람에게 길을 물으니 네 멋대로 가라 한다』(위즈덤하우스)

『그대 속눈썹에 걸린 세상』(북클라우드)

『당신이 좋아요 있는 그대로』(RHK 두앤비컨텐츠)

『낙타를 모는 성자』(호미출판사) 외 다수

2024 허허당 통일염원 초대전 고성 통일전망대

2024 허허당 그림콘서트 '접외풍경' 가나인사아트센터

2022 허허당 화엄세계 초대전 이웰갤러리

2017 허허당 초대전 제주도 심헌갤러리

2015 허허당 작품전 '바람의 기억' 가나인사아트센터

2014 허허당 초대전 육군3사관학교

2013 허허당 초대전 갤러리 한빛

2010 허허당이 본 화엄세계 하와이 전시

2009 '백만 동자(새벽)' 전국 순회음악회 서울 · 대구 · 부산

2008 '백만 동자(새벽)' 완성

2007 허허당이 본 화엄세계 '천년의 세월을 씻고' 초대전 불일미술관

2000 허허당이 본 화엄세계 '생명의 축제' 초대전 스위스 레제미드

1998 세계문화유산기념 초대전 합천 해인사

1997 허허당이 본 화엄세계 '우담바라의 꽃은 피고' 전국 순회전
         서울 공평아트홀, 부산 국제신문사, 광주 라인문화회관

1995 허허당이 본 화엄세계 '생명의 걸음으로' 서울역문화회관

1991 허허당 선화전 '가고 가고 또 간다' 벽아미술관

1984 허허당 선화전 '빈 마음의 노래' 중앙화랑